Creating Web Animations
Bringing Your UIs to Life

Kirupa Chinnathambi

Beijing · Boston · Farnham · Sebastopol · Tokyo

Creating Web Animations

by Kirupa Chinnathambi

Printed in the United States of America.

Published by O'Reilly Media, Inc., 1005 Gravenstein Highway North, Sebastopol, CA 95472.

O'Reilly books may be purchased for educational, business, or sales promotional use. Online editions are also available for most titles (*http://oreilly.com/safari*). For more information, contact our corporate/institutional sales department: 800-998-9938 or *corporate@oreilly.com*.

Editor: Meg Foley	**Indexer:** Angela Howard
Production Editor: Kristen Brown	**Interior Designer:** David Futato
Copyeditor: Rachel Monaghan	**Cover Designer:** Karen Montgomery
Proofreader: Molly Ives Brower	**Illustrator:** Rebecca Demarest

April 2017:   First Edition

Revision History for the First Edition
2017-03-15:   First Release

See *http://oreilly.com/catalog/errata.csp?isbn=9781491957516* for release details.

978-1-491-95751-6

[LSI]

Table of Contents

Preface

Animations are everywhere. Today, anything you do on a device with a screen is just one click, tap, or keystroke away from springing to life. As it turns out, animations are no longer a luxury or something to keep under wraps. Instead, they make up a large part of your experience using applications in your browser, on your phone, or on any other "smart" device. It's no surprise why. Users love animations. When done right, animations can make your applications easier to navigate, make your content more presentable, and even help your creations feel more alive and fun. Sometimes, animations look cool and you just gotta throw them in. These are all good things!™

What's the catch? Well, for all the great things animations have going for them, creating them is hard. On the web, the way you think about animations is different. The way you create them is also different...really different. The challenges that you once painfully overcame in older technologies like Flash are back in new and interesting ways. Fortunately, this is all part of learning something new. All you need is the right guide to help you along the way.

That guide is going to be me:

This is me.
This is me drinking bubble tea.
Bubble tea is my friend.

(This isn't a haiku)

Hi. My name is Kirupa, and I love animation. Ever since my parents bought me a computer in the early 1990s, I've been trying to get things to move on the screen and tell everybody how awesome it is. Nothing much has changed in my world since then…except for this book.

This book is all about teaching you how to create great animations for the web. It starts off with the very basics and gradually ratchets up the heat as you learn how to create more involved, more lifelike, and more complex animations. By the time you reach the last page, *you will have learned a lot about how to create animations in HTML, CSS, and JavaScript using the one-two punch of web standards and best practices.* If I did my job well, hopefully you had a bunch of fun along the way and laughed out loud a few times. More than likely, you will also have cringed a lot…kind of like you did after reading "one-two punch of web standards and best practices."

Know Your Basic HTML, CSS, and JavaScript

To get the most out of this book, you should be familiar with the basics of HTML, CSS, and JavaScript. By no means do I expect you to be an expert in any of these languages, but when you see some HTML or CSS or JavaScript, you should be able to understand what is going on with only a little handholding. This is the equivalent of knowing enough of a local language to get around town by reading the street signs.

If this doesn't describe you, shuffle (or push/click/flick/scroll) through this book and see how you feel after skimming through some of the pages. If most of what you see seems like unintelligible gibberish, then I encourage you to take a detour and learn the basics of working in HTML first. There are a lot of great books and online tutorials out there (hint: especially on *https://www.kirupa.com*), so you should be up and running very quickly. After that, you will probably have a much better time with this book.

About Authoring Tools

This entire book is written with no expectation that you use a fancy HTML authoring tool. A basic editor that allows you to see HTML, CSS, and JavaScript is all you need. If all you have is a text editor like Notepad, you'll be fine as well. This book is old school. It's all about manual labor and having you get your hands dirty when creating animations.

You may be wondering why a book aimed at teaching animation would avoid using animation tools. There are several reasons. The main one is that tools abstract away important details. They often make choices for you that you may not fully understand. When you're learning something new and complex such as web-based animations, I strongly believe that you need to know every single detail about what you are doing. That can only happen if you are fully involved in every part of what you are creating.

With all that said, once you've learned all about animations, their subtleties, and gotchas, take some time and look at the great tools that are out there. Well-designed tools help you to be significantly more productive than you ever will be defining animations by hand, and being productive is yet another good thing!™

Browser Support

Everything you learn in this book is designed to work on what all the cool people call a "modern" browser. That's just a fancy way of saying that if you are running a semirecent version of Chrome, Internet Explorer 11, Edge, Firefox, or Safari, you should be good to go. Also, before you ask, everything you see here will work beautifully on mobile devices like your iPhones, iPads, and Android-based gizmos!

Using the Code Examples

Supplemental material (code examples, exercises, etc.) is available for download at *https://github.com/kirupa/kirupa/tree/master/creating_web_animations*.

You will be seeing a fair amount of code in this book. Since I get a lot of questions regarding how you can use this code, the general gist is this: *for most "normal" cases, you can do whatever you want with the code without contacting me or O'Reilly.* That's a bit broad, so the following examples should help you out.

Situations where you don't need to ask for permission:

- Using the code from this book in your personal or commercial project
- Taking the code, modifying it, and sharing it with others
- Answering a question by using example code
- Printing out some code snippets and hanging them on your wall as an art installation

Situations where you need to ask for permission:

- Publishing a significant amount of this book's content and code
- Selling or distributing a CD-ROM (…or a VHS recording :P) of the examples you see
- Incorporating a significant amount of example code from this book into your product's documentation

If you feel your use of code examples falls outside fair use or the permission given above, feel free to contact us at *permissions@oreilly.com*.

O'Reilly Safari

 *Safari* (formerly Safari Books Online) is a membership-based training and reference platform for enterprise, government, educators, and individuals.

Members have access to thousands of books, training videos, Learning Paths, interactive tutorials, and curated playlists from over 250 publishers, including O'Reilly Media, Harvard Business Review, Prentice Hall Professional, Addison-Wesley Professional, Microsoft Press, Sams, Que, Peachpit Press, Adobe, Focal Press, Cisco Press, John Wiley & Sons, Syngress, Morgan Kaufmann, IBM Redbooks, Packt, Adobe Press, FT Press, Apress, Manning, New Riders, McGraw-Hill, Jones & Bartlett, and Course Technology, among others.

For more information, please visit *http://oreilly.com/safari*.

Getting Help/Contacting the Author

The last (and most important) thing to know before we get started is what to do when you get stuck or just need some assistance. The fastest and most effective way for getting help is to post on the forums at *http://forum.kirupa.com*. I or any of the many other friendly posters will help you out.

For any nontechnical assistance, you can contact me at *kirupa@kirupa.com*, tweet to *@kirupa*, or message me on Facebook (*http://facebook.com/kirupa*). I love hearing from readers like you, and I make it a point to personally respond to every message I receive.

Contacting O'Reilly

If you'd like to contact the publisher, then use the following details:

O'Reilly Media, Inc.
1005 Gravenstein Highway North
Sebastopol, CA 95472
800-998-9938 (in the United States or Canada)
707-829-0515 (international or local)

707-829-0104 (fax)

We have a web page for this book, where we list errata, examples, and any additional information. You can access this page at *http://bit.ly/creatingWebAnimations*.

To comment or ask technical questions about this book, send email to *bookquestions@oreilly.com*.

For more information about our books, courses, conferences, and news, see our website at *http://www.oreilly.com*.

Find us on Facebook: *http://facebook.com/oreilly*

Follow us on Twitter: *http://twitter.com/oreillymedia*

Watch us on YouTube: *http://www.youtube.com/oreillymedia*

Acknowledgments

Before we move on to the main part of the book, there are bunch of people that I'd like to thank for helping make this book a reality:

First, I'd like to thank *Meena*—my awesome wife who encouraged me to contact O'Reilly in the first place, helped get the ball rolling for the book you see right now, and patiently tolerated my antics (I am a writer, after all!) during the course of this book's writing.

Next, I'd like to thank *my parents* for always encouraging me to aimlessly wander and enjoy free time to do what I liked—such as spending a large amount of time on the computer trying to make pixels move around the screen. I wouldn't be half the rugged indoorsman/scholar/warrior I am today without them both.

On the publishing side, writing the words you see here is the easy part. Getting the book into your hands is an amazingly complex process. The more I learn about all the moving pieces involved, the more impressed I am at all the individuals who work tirelessly behind the scenes to keep this amazing machinery running. *To everyone at O'Reilly* who made this possible, thank you! There is one person I would like to explicitly call out: I'd like to thank *Meg Foley* for replying to my original email asking if I could write a book on web animations, patiently walking me through the publishing process, and working with me throughout to help make the book the best it can be. Next, I would like to thank Rachel Monaghan and Kristen Brown for turning the original draft of this book into a form of English that humans can easily understand. If the content in this book makes sense, a large amount of credit should be given to Rachel and Kristen for helping make that happen!

Lastly, the technical content of this book has been reviewed in great detail by my long-time friend and online collaborator, *Trevor McCauley (aka senocular)*. Words have not been invented (in any language…as far as I know) to express how grateful I am for his attention to detail and ability to highlight when I could explain something in a better, more clear way.

And with that…let's get started!

PART I

The Basics

Before you can create the totally awesome, cool, and useful animations that you want to create, we need to start at the beginning and cover the basics. We need to get a good feel for the building blocks you have at your disposal, not only for creating animations, but for creating animations that run really well. That sounds complicated, but as you will find out shortly, it's all pretty straightforward...for the most part. :P

In the following chapters, we are going to start at the very beginning and quickly ramp up to the important things you will need to learn and be aware of. That will set you up nicely for the rest of the book where we start applying everything we learned toward creating the animations that bring our UIs to life.

Onward!

CHAPTER 1

Introduction to Web Animations

While we think of animation as a recent creation brought about by film and computers, people have been fiddling with ways to communicate motion for a really *really* long time (Figure 1-1).

Figure 1-1. A sequence of pictures from 3000 BC (Wikipedia (http:// en.wikipedia.org/wiki/File:Vase_animation.svg))

Those ways have ranged from cave paintings and elaborate mechanical devices to more familiar, contemporary solutions, such as what you see on television, computers, and smartphones (Figure 1-2).

Figure 1-2. A really small sampling of apps that are lively and full of motion!

No longer are animations primarily in the domain of games, intros, cartoons, banner ads...or even cave paintings! Animations are deeply ingrained in today's technology, and they make up a large part of your applications' overall user experience. They can make your applications easier to navigate. They make your content more presentable. They can help your creations feel more alive and fun. Who doesn't want more of that?

That's enough background for now. You aren't here to get a history lesson or be convinced of why animations are useful. You probably already know about their importance. What you want to know is how to actually implement animations, and you have come to the right place. In this chapter and subsequent ones, you will learn how to work with animations in HTML. In a short time, you will become an animation expert...or at least be good enough to play one on TV.

What Is an Animation?

Before we proceed further down the bright, lava-filled pit where you learn how to create animations, let's take a step back and figure out what an animation is. Let's start with a definition. *An animation is nothing more than a visualization of change*—a change that occurs over a period of time.

Let's look at that definition in more detail.

The Start and End States

If visualizing change is an important part of an animation, we need to create some reference points so that we can compare what has changed. Let's call these reference points the *start* state and the *end* state. To better explain what is going on, let's come up with an easy-to-understand example as well.

Let's say our start state looks like Figure 1-3.

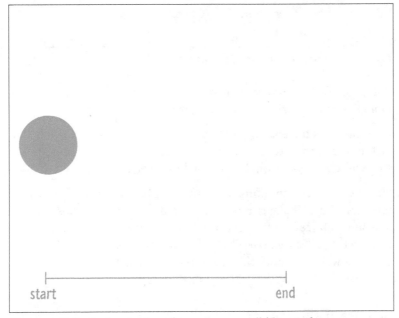

Figure 1-3. In the beginning, there was a small blue circle

You start off with a small blue circle located to the left of the screen. At the end state, your blue circle now looks sorta kinda like Figure 1-4.

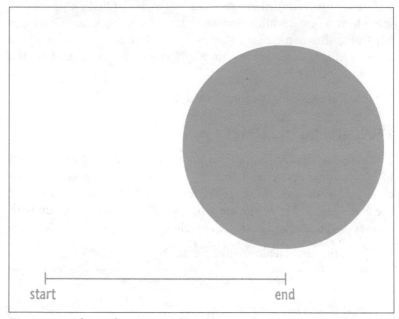

start   end

Figure 1-4. *The circle moves right and grows larger*

Based just on the information you have about what our blue circle looks like in the start and end states, what can you tell is different?

One change is the position. Our blue circle starts off on the left side of the screen. It ends up on the right side. Another change is the size. Our circle goes from being small to being much larger.

How do we make an animation out of this? If we were to just play the start and end states repeatedly, what you would see is a circle that just bounces from left to right very awkwardly. That is pretty turrible (*http://youtu.be/jKTb5Nfyh1o?t=38s*). Just turrible. What we need is a way to smooth things out between the start and end states. What we need is a healthy dose of *interpolation*.

Interpolation

Right now, what we have are two discrete states in time: the start state and the end state. If you were to play this back, it wouldn't be an animation. In order to make an animation out of what we have, we need a smooth transition that creates all the intermediate states. The process of creating these intermediate states is known as *interpolation*.

This interpolation, which occurs over a *period of time that you specify*, would look similar to Figure 1-5.

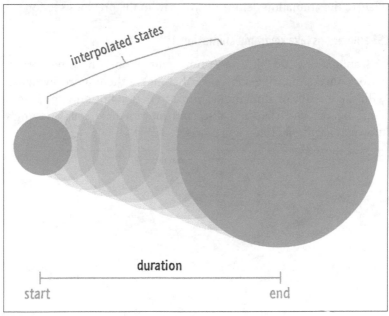

Figure 1-5. Behold...an animation!

You may be wondering who specifies the interpolated states. The answer, which is probably good news, is that your browser or HTML rendering engine will take care of the messy details. All you need to specify is the *start state*, the *end state*, and the *duration* over which the transition between the two states needs to occur. Once you have those three things, you have an animation!

Later you'll see how adding some other ingredients into the pot, such as timing functions (aka easing functions), can alter how the interpolation works. For now, though, just revel in this simple explanation of what makes up an animation, put on your best party clothes, and get ready to meet the three flavors of animation that you will end up using.

Animations on the Web

On the web, there isn't just a single animation implementation (hey, that sorta rhymes!) that you can use. You actually have three flavors of animation to choose from, and each one is specialized for certain kinds of tasks. Let's take a quick look at all three and see how they relate to the animation definition you saw in the previous section.

CSS animations (aka keyframe animations)

CSS animations are like traditional animations on some sort of performance-enhancing substance that makes them more awesome. With these kinds of animations, you can define not only the beginning and the end state but also any intermediate states, lovingly known as *keyframes* (see Figure 1-6).

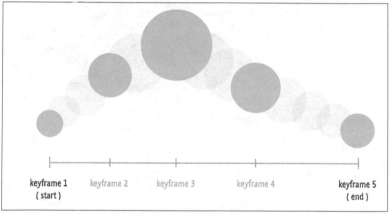

Figure 1-6. How an animation made up of keyframes might look

These intermediate states, if you choose to use them, give you greater control over the thing you are animating. In Figure 1-6, the blue circle isn't simply sliding to the right and getting larger. The individual keyframes adjust the circle's size and vertical position in ways that you wouldn't see if you simply interpolated between the start and end states.

Remember, even though you are specifying the intermediate states, your browser will still interpolate what it can between each state. Think of a keyframe animation as many little animations daisy-chained together.

CSS transitions

Transitions make up a class of animations where you only define the start state, end state, and duration. The rest, such as interpolating between the two states, is taken care of automatically for you (see Figure 1-7).

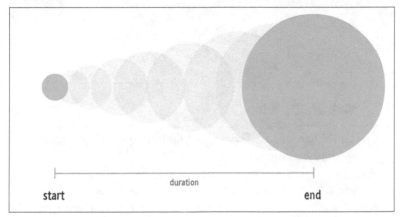

Figure 1-7. Transitions only need a start and end state to do their thing

While transitions seem like a watered-down, simplified keyframe animation, don't let that trick you. They are extremely powerful and probably the type of animation implementation you'll use the most.

Scripted/JavaScript animations

If you want full control over what your animation does right down to how it interpolates between states, you can use JavaScript (see Figure 1-8).

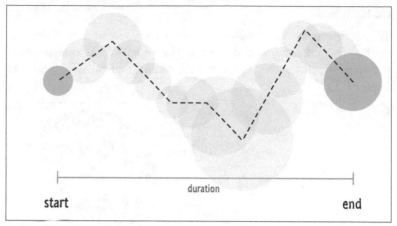

Figure 1-8. When you use JavaScript, you have a lot of freedom in defining how your animation works

There are a lot of cool things you can do when you opt out of the interpolation the browser does for you, but we won't be spending too much time in this area. Scripted animations have their place in games and visualizations, but covering those areas fully goes beyond the UI focus of this book.

Conclusion

To quickly recap, an animation is nothing more than a visualization of something changing over a period of time. In HTML, you have not one, not two, but *three* different ways of bringing animations to life: CSS animations, CSS transitions, and scripted animations (created in JavaScript). This book will primarily stay in the CSS-based world, and the following chapters will start you off right…I hope!

CHAPTER 2

Introduction to CSS Animations

When creating animations on the web, you can't really go far without running into CSS animations. What CSS animations do is pretty simple. They allow you to animate CSS properties by specifying what you want those properties to do at various points in time. These "points in time" are known as *keyframes*. If you've used animation tools in the past, the word "keyframes" should sound familiar to you. The keyframes you define in CSS as part of making your CSS animations work are the equivalent of the keyframes you would have visually defined in Flash/Animate, After Effects, or some other animation tool:

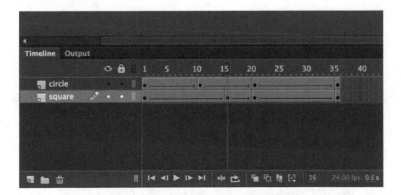

If you've never used animation tools in the past, don't worry. You won't be missing out on much. We'll be doing all of our animating manually (like an animal!) and learning what is going on at each step. By the end of this chapter, you'll have learned enough to create an animation made up of a smiling hexagon that bobs up and down.

Our hexagon will start off at the top:

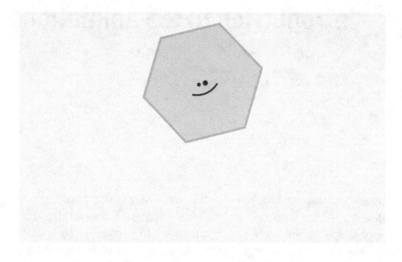

It will slide to the bottom:

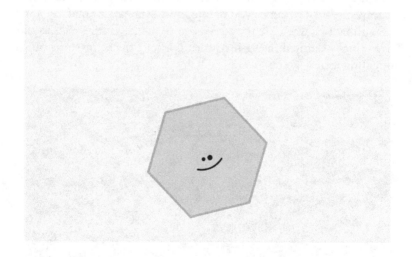

And at the end, our hexagon will slide back to the top:

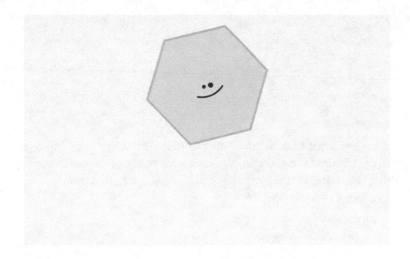

Along the way, we'll cover the `animation` property, the `@key frames` rule, and a handful of other topics that will set you up for cooler and more advanced techniques using CSS animations in the future.

Creating a Simple Animation

The easiest (and most fun!) way to learn about CSS animations is to just get your hands dirty with using them. Go ahead and create a new HTML document and add the following HTML and CSS to it:

```html
<!DOCTYPE html>
<html>

<head>
  <title>Intro to CSS Animations</title>

  <style>
    body {
      padding: 50px;
    }
    #container {
      padding: 20px;
      width: 100%;
      height: 250px;
      background-color: #EEE;
      text-align: center;
    }
  </style>
</head>
```

```
<body>
  <div id="container">
    <img id="hexagon"
         src="https://www.kirupa.com/images/hexagon.svg"/>
  </div>
</body>

</html>
```

Take a moment to look at what you just added. As web pages go, there isn't anything too complex or crazy going on here. The main thing to note is that we have an image element, and it has an id value of hexagon:

```
<div id="container">
  <img id="hexagon"
       src="https://www.kirupa.com/images/hexagon.svg"/>
</div>
```

We'll be coming back to this element in a little bit, so don't forget about it!

Now, before we move on to the next step, go ahead and preview this page in your browser. If everything worked right, you will see a happy hexagon shape…standing boringly still:

Let's fix the boredom by animating our hexagon shape. To do this, we are going to create a CSS animation. To create a CSS animation, you will need to complete two steps:

1. Set the `animation` property.
2. Define the keyframes that specify exactly how and when CSS properties get animated.

We'll tackle these steps one at a time. First, we'll deal with our `animation` property. In your style block where your style rules currently live, add the #hexagon style rule below your #container style rule:

```
#hexagon {
    animation: bobble 2s infinite;
}
```

The details of what is going on inside this style rule aren't important at the moment; we'll get acquainted with them later. For now, let's go to our next step and specify what our animation does by adding the keyframes. Add the following @keyframes style rule just below where your #hexagon style rule lives:

```
@keyframes bobble {
    0% {
        transform: translateY(10px);
    }
    50% {
        transform: translateY(40px);
    }
    100% {
        transform: translateY(10px);
    }
}
```

Once you've added this style rule, preview your page again. You should see your happy hexagon shape bobbing around happily as if it hasn't a care in the world. Awesome!

What Just Happened

You just defined a CSS animation that caused your hexagon shape to bobble around. In our rush to get the example working, though, we didn't stop to examine what exactly was going on at each step. We just ran screaming through it. So, let's take a few moments to revisit what we just did and learn more about why we did it.

The first thing we will look at is the `animation` property itself:

```
animation: bobble 2s infinite;
```

The `animation` property is responsible for setting your animation up. In the shorthand variant that you see (and will commonly use), you specify three values:

- The name of the animation
- The duration
- The number of times your animation will loop

You can see these values in our `animation` declaration. Our animation is called `bobble`, its duration is `2s` (seconds), and it is set to loop an `infinite` number of times.

As you can see, the `animation` declaration doesn't really contain much detail in terms of what gets animated. It sets the high-level definition of what your animation will do, but the actual substance of a CSS animation actually resides in its `@keyframes` rule.

Let's look at our `@keyframes` rule to learn more:

```
@keyframes bobble {
  0% {
    transform: translateY(10px);
  }
  50% {
    transform: translateY(40px);
  }
  100% {
    transform: translateY(10px);
  }
}
```

The first thing to notice is how our `@keyframes` rule is structured. On the outside, it contains the `@keyframes` declaration followed by a name:

```
@keyframes bobble {
  0% {
    transform: translateY(10px);
  }
  50% {
    transform: translateY(40px);
  }
  100% {
    transform: translateY(10px);
  }
}
```

On the inside, it contains style rules (aka the actual keyframes) whose selectors are percentage values (or the keywords `from` and `to`...but ignore that for now):

```
@keyframes bobble {
  0% {
    transform: translateY(10px);
  }
  50% {
    transform: translateY(40px);
  }
  100% {
    transform: translateY(10px);
  }
}
```

These style rules, often referred to as *keyframe style rules*, are pretty much what you would expect. They just contain CSS properties, such as `transform`, whose values will get applied when the rule becomes active.

Now, what I have just explained is the easy part. Here is where things could get a little bit confusing. Despite the `animation` property being declared in another style rule and your keyframes being declared in their own `@keyframes` rule, they are very much joined at the hip and one doesn't really function without the other being present.

So let's look at how the `animation` property and the `@keyframes` rule are tied together.

The Name

The name you give your `@keyframes` rule acts as an identifier that the `animation` property uses to know where the keyframes are:

```
#hexagon {
  animation: bobble 2s infinite;
}
@keyframes bobble {
  0% {
    transform: translateY(10px);
  }
  50% {
    transform: translateY(40px);
  }
  100% {
    transform: translateY(10px);
  }
```

```
    }
  }
```

It isn't a coincidence that our `animation` property refers to `bobble`, and the name of our `@keyframes` rule is also `bobble`. If there is ever an inconsistency in the names, your animation will not work.

Duration and Keyframes

So we now know how our `animation` property becomes aware of its keyframes—that solves one mystery. The next (and more complicated!) mystery is when a particular keyframe style rule actually becomes active.

As you recall, when you defined the keyframe style rules inside your `@keyframes` rule, our selector wasn't an actual time value. It was a percentage value:

```
@keyframes bobble {
  0% {
    transform: translateY(10px);
  }
  50% {
    transform: translateY(40px);
  }
  100% {
    transform: translateY(10px);
  }
}
```

What these values represent is the percentage of the animation that has completed. Using the values from our example, the 0% keyframe represents the start of our animation. The 50% keyframe represents our animation's midway point. And the 100% keyframe represents the end of our animation.

When we think of things happening in an animation, we don't think in terms of percentage values. We typically think in terms of points in time. To rationalize the differences between what CSS expects and what we humans expect, we need to understand the role the duration value plays. The duration value not only specifies the total length of our animation, it also helps specify the time at which a particular keyframe will become active.

Taking our 2-second-long animation as an example, the following diagram illustrates how our percentage values map to units of time:

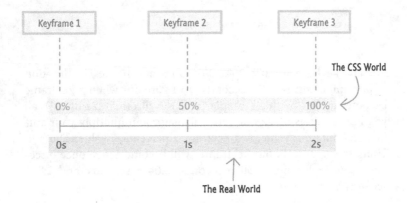

The Real World

The 0% keyframe becomes active at the beginning after 0 seconds have elapsed. The 50% keyframe becomes active after 1 second has elapsed. The 100% keyframe becomes active at the end, once 2 seconds have elapsed. Pretty simple, right? Right?!!

Calculating When a Keyframe Becomes Active for Nontrivial Cases

The math for figuring out when the 0%, 50%, and 100% keyframes for our 2-second animation work was pretty straightforward. You could probably figure out when those keyframes become active without breaking a sweat! The bad news is that you will run into situations where you can't figure out when a keyframe will play by just looking at it. For example:

```
#someWeirdShape {
    animation: blah 2.275s infinite;
}

@keyframes blah {
    0% {
        transform: translateY(10px);
    }
    25% {
        transform: translateY(20px);
    }
    33% {
        transform: translateY(80px);
    }
    90% {
        transform: translateY(30px);
    }
}
```

```
    100% {
        transform: translateY(10px);
    }
}
```

We have keyframes at 0%, 25%, 33%, 90%, and 100%. The duration of our animation is 2.275 seconds. To figure out when a keyframe becomes active for this example (and for all other examples!), all you have to do is break out your calculator and multiply your animation's duration value by a keyframe's percentage value. That's it. Using this approach, our keyframes will become active once 0 seconds, .56875 seconds, .75075 seconds, 2.0475 seconds, and 2.275 seconds have elapsed.

When I was learning about CSS animations for the first time, this was the confusing part. If you are still a bit confused, just remember that your keyframes have no concept of time. They only have a concept of percentage completed. The animation property with its duration value helps create the missing link between keyframes and time. Once you understand all of this, you will have jumped a major hurdle in being able to make sense of what your CSS animation is actually doing.

Looping

The third value you specify for the animation property determines the number of times your animation will play. You can specify an actual number, or you can specify the word infinite to have your animation play forever and ever...and ever! That's all there is to this value. Not particularly exciting, is it? :P

The Longhand Version

The animation property isn't always as concise as what we've seen here. There is a longhand variant where you can specify the animation-related properties individually. For our 2-second animation, it looks as follows:

```
#hexagon {
    animation-name: bobble;
    animation-duration: 2s;
    animation-iteration-count: infinite;
}
```

You use the `animation-name` property to specify the name of the `@keyframes` rule your animation relies on to run. You set your animation's duration with the `animation-duration` property, and you specify how many times you want the animation to loop with the `animation-iteration-count` property. There are a bunch more properties where these came from, and we'll cover all of them in a little bit.

Browser Support/Vendor Prefixes?

The `animation` property is pretty well supported (*http://caniuse.com/#feat=css-animation*) these days, so you don't need to use vendor prefixes (`-webkit-animation`, `-moz-animation`, etc.) in order to have it work across most browsers. If for whatever reason you need to support the very small number of users running older browsers, use a library like -prefix-free (*http://bit.ly/2m4zQLH*) to automatically deal with all of this vendor prefixing hullabaloo.

Conclusion

In this chapter, we've looked at how a simple CSS animation works. You learned all about how to declare an animation using the `anima tion` property and how the `@keyframes` rule with its keyframe style rules work. What we've seen is just a fraction of everything you can do with CSS animations, but it's the fraction you'll use almost all the time. What this means is that there are a bunch more animation-related properties with their own quirks that we didn't look at here. Instead of boring you with all of that now, I figure it is better for you to see them as part of examples that use them instead. You'll thank me later. Trust me. :P

CHAPTER 3

Introduction to CSS Transitions

When you're interacting with UIs, a lot of the animations you'll see won't be of the CSS animation kind (*https://www.kirupa.com/html5/introduction_css_animations.htm*) with its predefined keyframes. They will instead be reactions to the things you are doing. Examples of such reactions include a link underlining when you hover over it, a menu flying in when you tap on a button, or a text element getting bigger when it has focus. For animating these kinds of behaviors, you will use *CSS transitions*.

To better understand CSS transitions, let's take a moment to see one in action. In the following example, you'll see our friendly hexagon shape again. Initially, it will look like so:

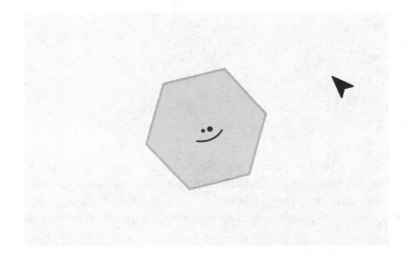

When you hover over it with your mouse, it will animate into this:

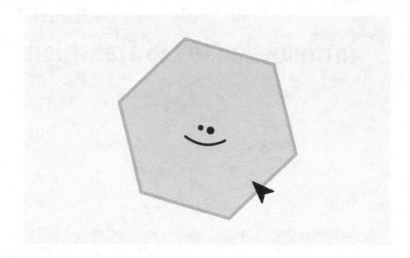

When your mouse is no longer on the hexagon, it returns to its normal self:

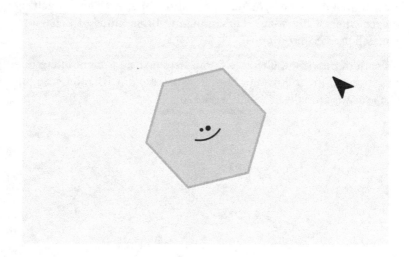

While it is hard to demonstrate how cool and awesome this is in a book, the image smoothly scales up and rotates when your mouse cursor is over it. It then smoothly scales and rotates back to its original state when your mouse cursor goes elsewhere. All of this is made possible thanks to the magic of CSS transitions, and in the following sections, you'll learn the basics of how to use them.

Creating a Simple Transition

Just like with CSS animations earlier, the way you'll learn about CSS transitions is simple. We are going to dive head first and just use them. The first thing we'll need to do is create a new HTML document and add the following things into it:

```html
<!DOCTYPE html>
<html>

<head>
  <title>CSS Transitions!</title>

  <style>
    #container {
      width: 100%;
      height: 290px;
      background-color: #EEE;

      display: flex;
      align-items: center;
      justify-content: center;
    }
  </style>
</head>

<body>
  <div id="container">
    <img id="hexagon"
         src="https://www.kirupa.com/images/hexagon.svg"/>
  </div>
</body>

</html>
```

After you've added all these lines of HTML and CSS, preview this document in your browser. If everything works correctly, you'll see an *almost* re-creation of the example you hovered over in the previous section:

It is an *almost* re-creation because hovering over our smiling hexagon does nothing. That's because we haven't added the CSS responsible for that yet. Before we do that, let's take a moment to see what we are dealing with. There's nothing crazy going on in the HTML and CSS you just added. The main detail you should notice is the markup used for displaying our hexagon image, which looks as follows:

```
<div id="container">
  <img id="hexagon"
       src="https://www.kirupa.com/images/hexagon.svg"/>
</div>
```

Now that we've gotten this out of the way, it's time to add our CSS and get our example moving—literally. What we want to do is have our hexagon image scale up and rotate when you hover over it. To make this happen, add the following CSS toward the bottom of your `style` block:

```
#hexagon:hover {
    transform: scale3d(1.2, 1.2, 1) rotate(45deg);
}
```

All we're doing is specifying a style rule that activates on hover (thanks to the `hover` pseudoclass). We set the `transform` property and call the `scale3d` and `rotate` functions that are responsible for scaling and rotating our hexagon image. Once you've added this CSS, preview this page in your browser and hover over the hexagon image. You'll see that the image now scales and rotates as expected. The only problem is that the scaling and rotating is not smooth and animated. The change is jarringly sudden!

To fix this, we are going to add a (you guessed it!) transition. Anywhere inside your `style` block, preferably before where we added our `#hexagon:hover` style rule, add the following style rule, which contains the `transition` property:

```
#hexagon {
  transition: transform .1s;
}
```

After you've added this style rule, preview your page again. This time, when you hover over your hexagon image, you'll see that it smoothly scales and rotates into place. W00t!!!

What Just Happened

In the previous section, we re-created the example we saw at the beginning by writing (or copying/pasting) some HTML and CSS. The end result was a hexagon image that scaled and rotated with a sweet transition when you hovered over it. The secret sauce that made our transition work is the very appropriately named `transition` property.

The way our `transition` property does its thing is pretty simple. *It animates property changes.* In order for it to do that, you need to specify just two things:

- The CSS property we want our transition to listen for changes on. You can use the keyword `all` if you want to listen to all property changes.
- How long the transition will run.

You can see how these things map to our `transition` that we have tucked away inside the `#hexagon` style rule:

```
transition: transform .1s;
```

We have our `transition` property; it is listening for changes to the `transform` property, and it runs for .1 seconds. We can see the result of this transition working when we hover over the hexagon image and change the `transform` property's value:

```
#hexagon:hover {
  transform: scale3d(1.2, 1.2, 1) rotate(45deg);
}
```

Our scale3d value goes from the default (1, 1, 1) to (1.2, 1.2, 1). Our rotate value goes from the default 0deg to 45deg. The CSS transition takes care of figuring out those intermediate, interpolated values to create the smooth animation you see over .1 seconds.

The Longhand Version

What we've seen so far is the transition shorthand variant. To specify a basic transition using just the longhand properties, you can set the transition-property and transition-duration properties as follows:

```
#hexagon {
  transition-property: transform;
  transition-duration: .1s;
}
```

The property names should be pretty self-explanatory. You specify the property you want your transition to act on with the transition-property property (or use a value of all to listen for all changes). You can set the transition-duration property to specify how long the transition will run. There are more transition-related properties that you'll need to know more about, but we'll deal with them later!

Conclusion

You've just learned the basics of how to define a simple CSS transition. Just knowing how to define a CSS transition by specifying the property to listen to and the transition duration will take you pretty far. But that's not good enough! For creating the kinds of more realistic animations that your UIs deserve and your users expect, there is actually a whole lot more for us to cover. We'll do all of that in subsequent chapters.

CHAPTER 4

Working with CSS Timing Functions

So far, we've created our animations and transitions by specifying only a handful of things: the properties to animate, the initial and final property values, and the duration. The exact syntax was different depending on whether we were dealing with a CSS animation or a transition, but the general ingredients were the same. The end result was an animation.

In this chapter, we are going to add one more ingredient into the mix. We are going to kick things up a few notches by using something known as a *timing function* (also referred to as an *easing function*). In the following sections, you're going to learn all about them!

What Is a Timing Function?

What a timing function is, or what it does, is a bit complicated to explain using just words. Before I confuse you greatly with the verbal explanation, take a look at the following example if you have a browser and internet connection handy: *http://bit.ly/timing_functions*.

What you see should look a little bit like the following:

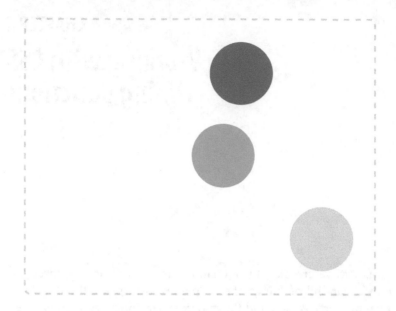

While the static image doesn't show all of this, in the live example there are three circles that start at the left, slide to the right, and return to where they started from. For all three of these circles, the key animation-related properties we've set are almost identical. They share the same duration, and the same properties are being changed by the same amount. You can observe that by noticing that the circles start and stop moving at the same time. Despite their similarities, though, the animation for each circle is obviously very different. What is going on here? How is this possible?

What's going on (and causing the difference in how each circle animates) is the star of this chapter: the timing function. Each circle's applied animation uses a different timing function to achieve the same goal of sliding the circles back and forth. So, let's get back to our original question: What exactly is a timing function? *A timing function is a function that alters the speed at which your properties animate.*

For example, your timing function could specify that your property values change linearly with time (Figure 4-1).

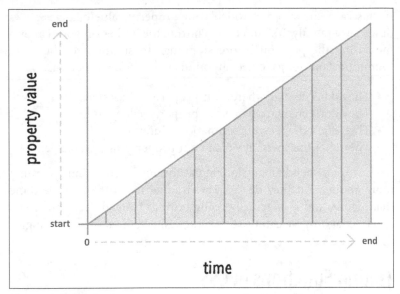

Figure 4-1. Boring!

This will result in your properties changing at a constant speed. If you want your property values to change in a more realistic way, you could throw in a timing function that mimics a deceleration, as in Figure 4-2.

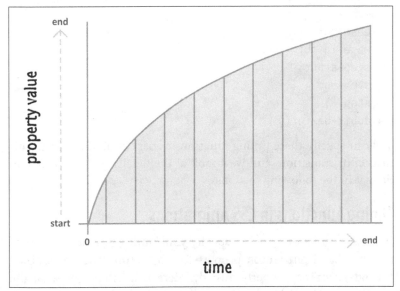

Figure 4-2. Much less boring!

In this case, the speed at which your property value changes slows down very rapidly. It's kind of like hitting the brakes on your car and measuring the position before stopping. To summarize, there are four important things to keep in mind about timing functions:

- They don't change where your property values start.
- They don't change where your property values end.
- They don't change your animation's duration.
- They alter the speed at which your property values change.

Now, we can spend all day looking at timing functions and learning more about what they do. We aren't going to do that. I have done that before, and it is actually really boring! Instead, let's shift gears and look at how we can use these magical creatures (I mean…ingredients) in CSS.

Timing Functions in CSS

Despite how complicated timing functions seem, using them in CSS is pretty straightforward. The various timing functions you can use are:

- `ease`
- `linear`
- `ease-in`
- `ease-out`
- `ease-in-out`
- `step-start`
- `step-end`
- `steps()`
- `cubic-bezier()`

You can specify these timing functions as part of defining your animation or transition, and we'll look at the details of how exactly to do that in the following sections.

Timing Functions in CSS Animations

In a CSS animation, you can specify your timing function as part of the shorthand `animation` property, or by setting the `animation-timing-function` property directly. Here is a snippet of what the shorthand and longhand variants might look like:

```
/* shorthand */
#foo {
  animation: bobble 2s ease-in infinite;
}

/* longhand */
#somethingSomethingDarkSide {
  animation-name: deathstar;
  animation-duration: 25s;
  animation-iteration-count: 1;
  animation-timing-function: ease-out;
}
```

When you declare your timing function as part of the animation
declaration, all of your keyframes will actually be affected by that
timing function value. For greater control, you can specify your timing functions on each individual keyframe instead:

```
@keyframes bobble {
  0% {
    transform: translate3d(50px, 40px, 0px);
    animation-timing-function: ease-in;
  }
  50% {
    transform: translate3d(50px, 50px, 0px);
    animation-timing-function: ease-out;
  }
  100% {
    transform: translate3d(50px, 40px, 0px);
  }
}
```

When you declare timing functions on individual keyframes, it
overrides any timing functions you may have set in the broader animation declaration. That is a good thing to know if you want to mix
and match timing functions and have them live in different places.

One last thing to note is that the animation-timing-function
declared in a keyframe only affects the path your animation will take
from the keyframe it is declared on until the next keyframe. This
means you can't have an animation-timing-function declared on
your end (aka 100%) keyframe because there is no "next keyframe."
If you do end up declaring a timing function on the end keyframe
anyway, that timing function will simply be ignored…and your
friends and family will probably make fun of you behind your back
for it.

Timing Functions in CSS Transitions

Transitions are a bit easier to look at since we don't have to worry about keyframes. Your timing function can only live inside the `tran sition` shorthand declaration or as part of the `transition-timing-function` property in the longhand world:

```
/* shorthand */
#bar {
    transition: transform .5s ease-in-out;
}

/* longhand */
#karmaKramer {
    transition-property: all;
    transition-duration: .5s;
    transition-timing-function: linear;
}
```

There really isn't anything more to say. As CSS properties go, transitions are pretty easy to deal with!

Default Timing Function Values

Specifying a timing function as part of your animation or transition is optional. The reason is that every animation or transition you use has its `timing-function` property defined by default with a value of `ease`.

Meet the Timing Function Curve

Timing functions are very visual creatures. While we use them in terms of their CSS names (`ease`, `ease-in`, etc.), the way we'll commonly run into them is visually through something known as a *timing function curve* (see Figure 4-3).

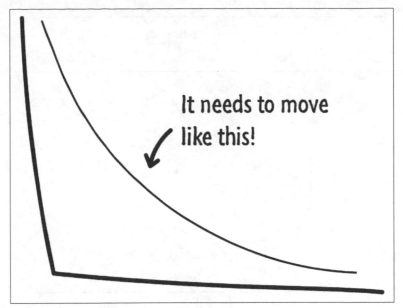

Figure 4-3. An example of a timing function curve

The timing function curve isn't a generic representation for all timing functions. Each timing function has a very specific timing function curve associated with it. Figure 4-4 shows the timing function curves look like for the predefined CSS timing functions.

You can sorta see from Figure 4-4 how the different timing functions end up affecting how our animation runs.

Now, there are two timing functions that we did not include in Figure 4-4: `steps` and `cubic-bezier`. These timing functions are *special* (which is usually code for complicated)! We will look at each in more detail in the following sections.

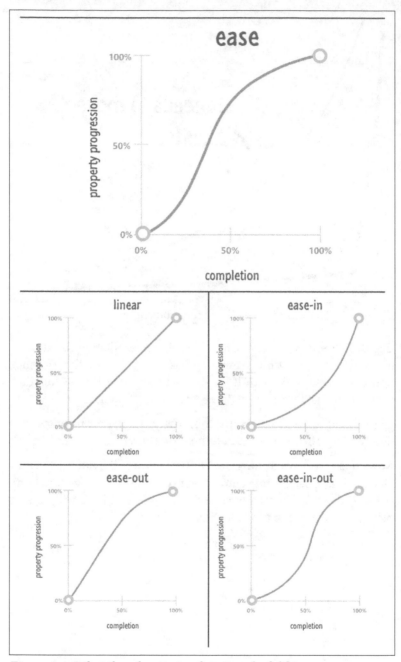

Figure 4-4. What the other timing functions look like

The cubic-bezier Timing Function

The cubic-bezier timing function is the most awesome of the timing functions we have. The way it works is a little complicated. It takes four numbers as its argument:

```
.foo {
    transition: transform .5s cubic-bezier(.70, .35, .41, .78);
}
```

These four numbers define precisely how our timing function will affect the property that is getting animated. With the right numerical values, you can re-create all of our predefined timing functions (like ease, ease-in-out, etc.). Now, that's not particularly interesting. What is really *really* interesting is the large variety of custom timing functions that you can create instead.

For example, with the cubic-bezier timing function you can create a timing function that looks like Figure 4-5.

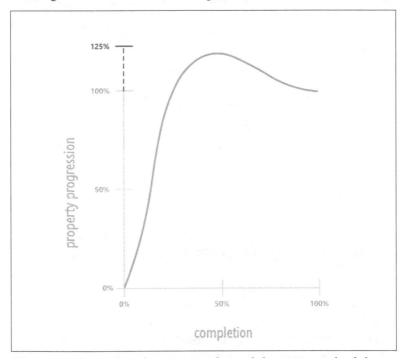

Figure 4-5. This timing function goes beyond the 100% mark while running

What this timing function highlights is that your property value will animate a bit beyond its final target and then snap back! That is something you can't do using the predefined timing functions. This is just the tip of the iceberg on the kinds of timing functions you can create.

Now, you are probably wondering how we figure out the four numbers to throw into the cubic-bezier timing function. It's one thing to look at a timing function curve and make sense of what is going to happen. It is quite another to look at four boring numbers to make sense of the same things. Fortunately, we'll never have to calculate the four numbers ourselves. There are a handful of online resources that allow us to visually define the timing function curve, which, in turn, generates the four numerical values that correspond to it.

My favorite of those online resources is Lea Verou's cubic-bezier generator (*http://cubic-bezier.com/*):

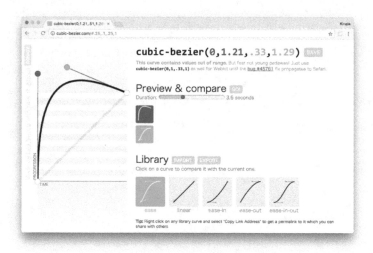

You can use this generator to easily create a timing function by defining the timing function curve, previewing what an animation using that timing function would look like, and getting the numerical values that you can plug into your markup. Pretty simple, right?

The step Timing Function

The last timing function we will look at affects the rate at which our properties change but isn't technically a timing function. This "non-timing function thing" is known as a *step timing function* (see Figure 4-6).

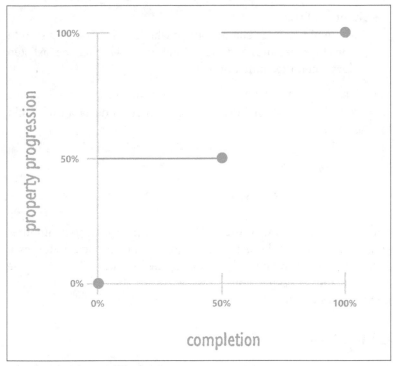

Figure 4-6. The step timing function

What a step function does is pretty unique. It allows you to play back your animation in fixed intervals. For example, in the step function graph in Figure 4-6, your animated property progression starts at 0%. At the 50% mark, it jumps to 50%. At the end of the animation, your property progression reaches 100%. There is no smooth transition between the various frames or "steps." The end result is a bit jagged.

In CSS, you can define the step function by using the appropriately named steps function:

```
.pictureContainer img {
  position: relative;
  top: 0px;
  transition: top 1s steps(2, start);
}
```

The steps function takes two arguments:

- Number of steps
- A value of start or end to specify whether the first step should occur at the beginning of the animation or whether the last step occurs when the animation ends

For example, if I want my animation to have five steps and have a step when the animation ends, my steps function declaration would look as follows:

```
.pictureContainer img {
  position: relative;
  top: 0px;
  transition: top 1s steps(5, end);
}
```

One thing to note is that, the more steps you specify, the smoother your animation will be. After all, think of an individual step as a frame of your animation. The more frames you have over the same duration, the smoother your final result will be. That same statement applies for steps as well.

Conclusion

The icing on your animation- or transition-flavored cake is the timing function. The type of timing function you specify determines how lifelike your animation will be. By default, you have a handful of built-in timing functions you can specify as part of the animation-timing-function or transition-timing-function properties for your CSS animations and transitions. Whatever you do, just don't forget to specify a timing function! The default ease timing function isn't a great substitute for some of the better ones you can use, and your animation or transition will never forgive you for it.

Also, before I forget, here is the full markup for the three sliding circles that you saw at the beginning of the chapter:

```
<style>
  .circle {
```

```
      width: 100px;
      height: 100px;
      border-radius: 50%;
      margin: 30px;
      animation: slide 5s infinite;
    }
    #circle1 {
      animation-timing-function: ease-in-out;
      background-color: #E84855;
    }
    #circle2 {
      animation-timing-function: linear;
      background-color: #0099FF;
    }
    #circle3 {
      animation-timing-function: cubic-bezier(0, 1, .76, 1.14);
      background-color: #FFCC00;
    }
    #container {
      width: 550px;
      background-color: #FFF;
      border: 3px #CCC dashed;
      border-radius: 10px;
      padding-top: 5px;
      padding-bottom: 5px;
      margin: 0 auto;
    }
    @keyframes slide {
      0% {
        transform: translate3d(0, 0, 0);
      }
      25% {
        transform: translate3d(380px, 0, 0);
      }
      50% {
        transform: translate3d(0, 0, 0);
      }
      100% {
        transform: translate3d(0, 0, 0);
      }
    }
  </style>

<div id="container">
  <div class="circle" id="circle1"></div>
  <div class="circle" id="circle2"></div>
  <div class="circle" id="circle3"></div>
</div>
```

There is nothing crazy going on in this example, so I'll leave you to
it...and see you in the next chapter!

CHAPTER 5

Ensuring Your Animations Run Really Smoothly

For the longest time, creating smooth and highly performant animations using only web technologies was very difficult. The browsers were slow, CSS properties weren't optimized for rapid updates, the graphics card didn't do much work, you had to walk 15 miles in the snow to get to school, and so on (see Figure 5-1).

You remember those days, right?

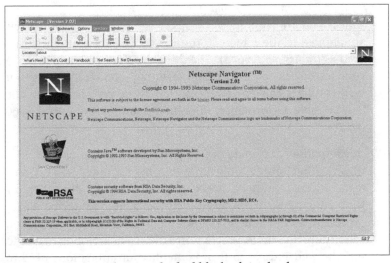

Figure 5-1. What a browser looked like back in the day

Fortunately, nowadays those problems have mostly gone away. While you still might have to walk 15 miles to get to school (in the snow, barefoot, wolves chasing you, etc.), our browsers have gotten really good about helping ensure our animations don't jitter, lag, tear, or exhibit any other unwanted visual side effects that are jarring to see.

Now, this doesn't mean we can pack our bags and go home. Our browsers provide you with all the controls to create animations that run well, but you need to know which controls to fiddle with. Don't worry—that's where this chapter comes in! In the following sections, you'll learn how to ensure your animations run really *really* well.

What Is a Smooth Animation?

Before we start digging into the code, let's step back for a moment and clarify what we mean by a *smooth animation*. At a high level, there are three major things smooth animations have going for them:

They are responsive.
    The time between your triggering an animation (by clicking, tapping, dragging, etc.) and your animation starting to do something is as short (~100 ms) as possible.

They run at 60 frames per second (fps).
    Unless you are running some space-age hardware, your pixels are painted to the screen 60 times a second (commonly measured as *frames per second*). The things you animate and paint to your screen can't go higher than that magical 60 fps number, but they certainly can go lower—noticeably lower! To ensure the best possible performance, smooth animations always run at 60 fps.

They are responsive (#1) and fast (#2) on mobile devices.
    It's one thing for your animation to run awesomely well on your high-powered dev machine. It is another thing altogether for your animation to run awesomely on a mobile device where processor, memory, and graphics capabilities are less abundant. With more and more people primarily using a mobile device to surf the web and get to their content, your animations need to run well on them too.

These three criteria may look a bit scary, but as you will see in a little bit, there are just a few tips you need to keep in mind to easily ensure your animations run as smooth as butter:

Butter! Not butter croissant :P

Anyway, with all this said, let's roll up our sleeves and look at how exactly we are going to accomplish all of this.

Creating Responsive 60 fps Animations

To create animations that are responsive and run at 60 fps, there are two things you should do:

- Primarily animate CSS properties that we'll call *animation-friendly*. These are properties that are optimized heavily for rapid changes and screen updates.
- Offload work to the GPU (aka the graphics card) where things like animations can be handled much better than your less-optimal-for-visual-stuff CPU.

Now that you have an idea of what to expect, it's time to get technical and learn some new CSS techniques along the way.

Meet the Animation-Friendly Properties

Your browser can animate certain types of CSS properties really efficiently. We'll call these the animation-friendly properties, and they are transform, opacity, and filter. Limiting the properties you can animate to just these three may seem a bit odd, but take a look at everything you can do with them:

transform
> This property allows you to change an element's position using the translate function, make it bigger/smaller using the scale function, set a rotation using the...um...rotate function, and skew the element using the skew function.

opacity
> This property allows you to adjust an element's transparency.

filter
> This property allows you to apply visual effects such as drop shadows, glows, color corrections, and more to your elements.

As you can see, you can do quite a lot with these properties. Now, you are probably wondering what it is about these three properties that makes them special. The full answer for that requires looking at browser internals and how pixels make it onto the screen. That goes a bit beyond what we need to focus on right now, but the short answer is that *these properties make your browser do the least amount of work to get visual updates to the screen.* If our goal is to have these visual updates appear 60 times a second, the less time your browser spends doing unnecessary work, the more easily it can stay at the 60 fps mark.

Now, before we wrap this section up, there is one really important thing to mention. There will be times when what you are trying to animate can't be represented by transform, opacity, and filter. During those times, it is totally OK to animate the other CSS properties. For example, animating an element's color is a common scenario, and there is nothing wrong with using the color or background-color properties for that task. The transform, opacity, and filter properties can be used to represent many animation-oriented scenarios, but don't try to force their use when another CSS property would be better. Use your judgment on that.

Don't Animate margin, top, left, and So On!

For animation purposes, unless you have a specific need, you absolutely should not animate the margin, padding, top, left, bottom, or right CSS properties. That's right...I said it! Since you probably use these properties a lot for various positioning-related tasks, I know this may sound a bit counterintuitive. The reason for my seemingly heretical stance has to do with performance. Let me explain...

Each time you modify the value set on these properties (and other layout-impacting properties like it), your browser does extra work to calculate how the modifications *affect the layout of your entire document*. I am not against you using these properties to help with your layout. Using these properties infrequently as part of a document load or resize is fine. Using these properties and modifying their values 60 times a second as part of an animation or transition is definitely not great. Calculating and recalculating the elements in your page is one of the most expensive operations your browser can do.

You could choose to set the position property of the elements you are animating to fixed or absolute. That avoids your browser having to calculate the layout for your entire document. While this is a better optimization, your browser still has to do unnecessary layout-related calculations on the element that is moving as part of figuring out the box model. Sigh.

For best results, keep things simple and just change the transform property when trying to change an element's position.

Push Element Rendering to the GPU

Animating elements is a very visual and graphics-heavy operation. It would seem reasonable that they would primarily render on your *GPU* instead of the CPU, which juggles a billion different things, right? The answer is obviously yes. Too bad that doesn't match reality. Whether your animated elements render on the GPU or CPU depends on the CSS property you are modifying, the device you are viewing the animation on, and what each browser decides to do.

You can avoid all of this uncertainty by clearly telling your GPU to take some initiative and render the elements that need to be animated.

While that sounds complicated, it is actually fairly straightforward. You do this by setting a `translate3d` (or `translateZ`) transform on the elements you want your GPU to handle.

Here is an example of what this looks like:

```
#slidePanel {
    transform: translate3d(0, 0, 0);
}
```

By doing this, we've pushed the rendering of the `slidePanel` element entirely to the graphics card. This means your animations on the `slidePanel` element will render on something dedicated to ensuring they run smoothly.

This seems like an awesome trick to ensuring smooth animations, right? Well, it does...but as with all awesome tricks, you need to use it responsibly.

Minimize the elements you want the GPU to deal with

Push only to the elements you will be animating to the GPU. For every element that you send to the GPU, your browser will spend time and video memory (on your GPU) to store the element. The fewer elements you *optimize* in this way, the better off you will be.

Also, while it goes without saying, resist the temptation to do this:

```
* {
    transform: translate3d(0, 0, 0);
}
```

This tells your browser to push every element to your GPU! For the performance and memory reasons mentioned earlier, you *definitely* shouldn't do this.

Give your browser a chance to push an element to the GPU

Pushing an element to the GPU at the same time you are about to animate properties on it is not a good idea. Take a look at the following snippet:

```
#blah {
    transition: all .2s ease-in-out;
    background-color: #FFF;
}
#blah:hover {
    transform: translate3d(0, 0, 0);
```

```
    background-color: #EEE;
  }
```

When we hover over the blah element, we animate the background-color property from #FFF to #EEE. To ensure the blah element's rendering is hardware-accelerated, we use our translate3d trick inside the style rule where the hover takes place:

```
#blah {
  transition: all .2s ease-in-out;
  background-color: #FFF;
}
#blah:hover {
  transform: translate3d(0, 0, 0);
  background-color: #EEE;
}
```

While that seems like a good idea, *it really is not.* By the time your element is transferred to the GPU, your browser will have already started to animate the transform property. Any optimizations you might have hoped to gain would be lost.

The right behavior is to pick a time prior to when your element's properties are about to get animated and push the element to the GPU at that time. The easiest time is during page load, but you can optimize for a later time if you can better predict when the user will trigger an animation. Here is what a revised version of our example would look like:

```
#blah {
  transition: all .2s ease-in-out;
  background-color: #FFF;
  transform: translate3d(0, 0, 0);
}
#blah:hover {
  background-color: #EEE;
}
```

This time, when our page loads and our styles are processed, our blah element is pushed to the GPU. This ensures that whenever the blah element is hovered over, there is no doubt about where the rendering is taking place—it's in GPU country!

What Is This Magical will-change Property?

At the end of the day, our browser knows more than we do about which elements to optimize and when the right time to optimize those elements is. We can do our best to proactively predict and do the right thing, but we will always be left wondering whether we second-guessed the browser or not. We can sort of see this with the various caveats each of our awesome tricks came with. None of them was a slam dunk that guaranteed your animations would run really smoothly.

The newish will-change property can help solve this. This property allows you to tell your browser which properties you'd like to animate, and its usage looks a little bit like this:

```
.square {
  width: 450px;
  height: 450px;

  animation: robotSlide .2s linear;
  will-change: transform, opacity;
}

@keyframes robotSlide {
  0% {
    transform: translate(10px, 10px);
    opacity: 1;
  }
  50% {
    transform: translate(100px, 10px);
    opacity: .5;
  }
}
```

Your browser uses the information you provide to figure out the best way to optimize your elements. It saves you from having to do any extra work, and the end result might be rendering the element on the GPU—or it might not, if the browser determines that doing so might result in worse performance. Your browser might even have some secret optimization that only it can pull off. That's the nice thing about just letting the browser deal with all of this animation optimization business.

The will-change property seems like the perfect solution we've all been looking for, right? Why is this not the first (and only) thing we learn about in this chapter? That's where the bad news comes in. This property is fairly new, and browser support is still spotty. Some of the major browsers don't even support it. How exactly it figures out what optimizing magic to do, and when, is something that still isn't fully understood. Until all of those things change, you should be cautious about using this property...no matter how awesome it sounds.

Conclusion

Phew! Who knew that animating a handful of elements has so much performance-related backstory and intrigue? The main takeaway here is that you need to do just two things to create really perform-ant and smooth animations:

- Use the animation-friendly properties of `transform`, `opacity`, and `filter` as much as possible.
- Responsibly push elements you are animating to get rendered by the GPU.

As long as you do these two things, your animations will be respon-sive, run blazingly fast at 60 fps, and look good on mobile devices as well. What more could we ask for? Maybe this totally sweet image:

CHAPTER 6

Transitions, Animations, and JavaScript

So far, while learning the basics of how CSS animations and transitions work, we haven't deviated too far from the safe middle road. We loaded the page, and an animation automatically started to play. We hovered over an element, and some property on that element animated in some way. The middle road is fine for many cases, but there is so much more we can do. In this chapter, we are going to take some less beaten paths and expand the ways we can interact with animations and transitions by adding in a dash of JavaScript.

By adding JavaScript, we can start to do a lot more things, such as:

- Having our animations play at a time other than during page load or in response to simple gestures like hover, focus, and so on.
- Defining the properties we animate, their values, or both on the fly as opposed to having them always be predefined in our CSS.
- Having the element whose properties we animate be wildly different than the element we trigger the animation on.

These are all situations that you'll run into frequently, and they also are situations that you simply can't bring to life using only CSS. You need to involve JavaScript, and this chapter will show you some of the ways you can do that. Also, don't worry if you are not a JavaScript expert. We'll stay out of the complex stuff as much as possible, but we will review a few key JavaScript concepts that you will see over and over again as you go about creating animations.

It's Just Property Changes

As you've heard a billion times by now, our animations work off of property changes. Our properties start off with a value, a few moments go by, and our properties animate to a new value. Now, here is the important detail about all of this. *Our browser does not care where the various values for an animated property come from.* As long as they come from somewhere, everything is golden. This little detail makes up the cornerstone of how JavaScript, animations, and transitions can work well together.

The Example

The best way to make sense of what all of this means is to look at an example. Let's say that you have a rectangle that looks like this:

If we were to click or tap anywhere inside this rectangle, the rectangle's color will change:

This color change won't be sudden—at least not on our computers when we create this in a few moments. The color will animate to its new value. As you keep clicking or tapping on the rectangle, you will see another background color animate into view. You can do this all day, as the background colors are randomly generated thanks to some help from our old friend, JavaScript.

Initial State Using CSS, Changes Using JS

This example follows a pattern that you will use frequently when working with animations using both CSS and JavaScript. The pattern loosely looks like:

1. Define the initial state using CSS.
2. Make changes using JavaScript.

Let's see how this pattern applies to our random color example. First, create a new HTML document and add the following HTML, CSS, and JavaScript into it:

```
<!DOCTYPE html>
<html>

<head>
    <title>Changing Color</title>
</head>

<body>

<style>
    #container {
        width: 75%;
        height: 290px;
        cursor: pointer;
        box-shadow: 0px 0px 15px #CCC;
        border-radius: 10px;
        margin: 0 auto;
        background-color: yellow;
        transition: background-color .2s ease-out;
    }
</style>

<div id="container">

    <script>
      var container = document.querySelector("#container");
      var zeros = "0000000";

      container.addEventListener("click", changeColor, false);

      function changeColor(e) {
          var color = "#" + Math.floor(Math.random() *
                                      0xFFFFFF).toString(16);
```

```
        var colorLength = color.length;

        if (colorLength < 7) {
            color += zeros.substring(0, zeros.length - colorLength);
        }
        container.style.backgroundColor = color;
    }
    </script>
</div>
</body>

</html>
```

Take a few moments to understand what is going on. Once you've done that, read on! In the following sections, we'll look at each of the interesting things we see here in more detail.

Initial state and CSS

When you first saw the example, you saw a yellow rectangle. The markup behind it isn't too crazy. The HTML for it is just a div element with an id value of container:

```
<div id="container"></div>
```

The more interesting stuff is in the CSS, and it looks as follows:

```
#container {
    width: 75%;
    height: 290px;
    cursor: pointer;
    box-shadow: 0px 0px 15px #CCC;
    border-radius: 10px;

    background-color: yellow;
    transition: background-color .2s ease-out;
}
```

Take a moment to look through the various CSS properties being set and their values. Most of them just deal with our rectangle's appearance, but we do define our transition property where we listen for changes to the background-color property and animate any change over a duration of .2s with an ease-out.

Changes and JavaScript

Our rectangle (aka our `container`) element's background color changes every time we click on it. That is handled entirely via the following lines of JavaScript:

```
var container = document.querySelector("#container");
var zeros = "0000000";

container.addEventListener("click", changeColor, false);

function changeColor(e) {
    var color = "#" + Math.floor(Math.random() *
                            0xFFFFFF).toString(16);
    var colorLength = color.length;

    if (colorLength < 7) {
      color += zeros.substring(0, zeros.length - colorLength);
    }
    container.style.backgroundColor = color;
}
```

The `container` property stores a reference to our `container div` element. When we click on this element, we call the `changeColor` function that is responsible for generating a random color and setting it. All of that is well and fine, but the line of code that is really important for the animation we eventually see is the following:

```
container.style.backgroundColor = color;
```

In this line, we are setting our `container` element's background color to the new, randomly generated value. Changing our background color here starts our transition (defined earlier in CSS and applied on the same `container` element) and animates the background color property to the new value.

What Just Happened?

In the previous few sections, we walked through an example where our background color animated to a new value each time you clicked/tapped. The reason why the animation works is pretty simple, but it is worth repeating in slightly more detail here.

In the CSS that applies to our `container` element, we defined our transition where we listen for changes to the background-color property:

```
#container {
    width: 75%;
    height: 290px;
    cursor: pointer;
    box-shadow: 0px 0px 15px #CCC;
    border-radius: 10px;
    background-color: yellow;
    transition: background-color .2s ease-out;
}
```

In our JavaScript, we have some code that changes the background color on the same `container` element:

```
container.style.backgroundColor = color;
```

Because our transition is listening for background color changes on the `container` element and our JavaScript is changing the background color on the same `container` element, the result is an animation from one background color value to another.

To us, defining styles in CSS and changing them via JavaScript to trigger an animation seems out of this world. To our browser, it is just business as usual. See, our browser doesn't really care how CSS properties and their values find their way onto an element. That is because they only care about something known as the *computed style* (see Figure 6-1).

What you see here is the computed style for our `container` element; notice the properties and the values set on it. You can see our `tran sition` property (entirely in longhand), the `background-color` property, and a bunch of other properties that detail other aspects of how this element looks. This is why our example works as well as it does. From our browser's point of view, the computed value for the background color changes. It doesn't matter that it changes via JavaScript. The end result is that the background color changes and a transition is listening for changes on it.

| Styles | Computed | Event Listeners | DOM Breakpoints | Properties |

Filter   ☐ Show all

▶ background-color	☐ rgb(255, 255, 0)
▶ border-bottom-left-radius	10px
▶ border-bottom-right-radius	10px
▶ border-top-left-radius	10px
▶ border-top-right-radius	10px
▶ box-shadow	■ rgb(204, 204, 204) 0px…
▶ cursor	pointer
▶ display	block
▶ height	290px
▶ transition-delay	0s
▶ transition-duration	0.2s
▶ transition-property	background-color
▶ transition-timing-function	ease-out
▶ width	1025.25px

Figure 6-1. The Computed tab in the Chrome Dev Tools is a great way to figure out what style properties are set and their values

A Tale of Two Styling Approaches

By now, this should come as no surprise to you. Setting CSS properties and changing the values on them is something you'll need to know how to do as part of creating animations. If you are familiar with all of this, feel free to skip on to the next section. If you aren't familiar with this, then read on.

When it comes to setting CSS styles using JavaScript, you have two options:

- Setting a CSS property directly on the element. (We kinda saw this already when we set the background color earlier).
- Adding or removing class values from an element, which may result in certain style rules getting applied or ignored.

Let's look at both of these cases in greater detail, as we'll use these techniques in many of the animations we'll be dealing with in the future.

Setting the Style Directly

Every HTML element that you access via JavaScript has a `style` object. This object allows you to specify a CSS property and set its value. For example, here we set the background color of an HTML element whose `id` value is `superman`:

```
var myElement = document.querySelector("#superman");
myElement.style.backgroundColor = "#D93600";
```

To affect many elements, you can do something like this:

```
var myElements = document.querySelectorAll(".bar");

for (var i = 0; i < myElements.length; i++) {
  myElements[i].style.opacity = 0;
}
```

In a nutshell, to style elements directly using JavaScript, first we have to access the element. We're using the `querySelector` (*http://bit.ly/2n4fwPo*) method to do that. The second step is just to find the CSS property you care about and give it a value. Remember, many values in CSS are actually strings. Also remember that many values require a unit of measurement, like `px` or `em`, to actually get recognized.

Special-Casing Some Names of CSS Properties

JavaScript is very picky about what makes up a valid property name. Most names in CSS would get JavaScript's seal of approval, so you can just use them straight from the carton. There are a few things to keep in mind, though.

To specify a CSS property in JavaScript that contains a dash, the tried-and-true approach is to simply remove the dash and capitalize the first letter of each word that follows the first. For example, `background-color` becomes `backgroundColor`, `border-radius` becomes `borderRadius`, and so on.

A newer approach is to ignore all of this and just use array access:

```
el.style["background-color"] = "#FFFFFF";
```

I'm old school, so I prefer the first approach. If you are going to rely on array access, make sure to test on any older browsers you may care about.

Also, certain words in JavaScript are reserved and can't be used directly. One example of a CSS property that falls into this special

---

category is float. In CSS it is a layout property. In JavaScript, it stands for something else. To use a property whose name is entirely reserved, prefix the property with css (so float becomes cssFloat).

Adding and Removing Classes Using JavaScript

The second way of setting CSS styles using JavaScript involves adding and removing class values that, in turn, change which style rules get applied. For example, let's say you have the following style rule:

```
.disableMenu {
    display: none;
}
```

In HTML, you have a menu whose id is dropDown:

```
<ul id="dropDown">
    <li>One</li>
    <li>Two</li>
    <li>Three</li>
    <li>Four</li>
    <li>Five</li>
    <li>Six</li>
</ul>
```

Now, if we wanted to apply our .disableMenu style rule to this element, all you would need to do is add disableMenu as a class value to the dropDown element:

```
<ul class="disableMenu" id="dropDown">
    <li>One</li>
    <li>Two</li>
    <li>Three</li>
    <li>Four</li>
    <li>Five</li>
    <li>Six</li>
</ul>
```

To accomplish the same result using JavaScript, we are going to use the classList API (*https://www.kirupa.com/html5/using_the_class list_api.htm*). This API makes it dirt simple to add or remove class values from an HTML element. To add the disableMenu class name to our dropDown element, use the add method on the HTML element's classList property:

```
var theDropDown = document.querySelector("#dropDown");
theDropDown.classList.add("disableMenu");
```

To remove the the `disableMenu` class name, we can call the `class List` API's remove method:

```
var theDropDown = document.querySelector("#dropDown");
theDropDown.classList.remove("disableMenu");
```

That's all there is to working with class values in JavaScript, but that isn't all there is to the `classList` API. If you are feeling especially bored, there is a whole lot more you can do with the `classList` API beyond just adding and remove class values. To see the `class List` API and all of its hobbies described in greater detail, check out the post "Using the classList API" (*https://www.kirupa.com/html5/using_the_classlist_api.htm*) on my website.

What About CSS Animations?

Here is a difficult truth that I want to share with you before we wrap things up: CSS animations can't be used easily with all of the JavaScript stuff we have been talking about. The reason has to do with how CSS animations are defined. The `animation` property by itself contains very little that you may want to modify using Java-Script outside of when it starts and stops. All of the interesting stuff a CSS animation does is defined by its keyframes. Here is the problem: *accessing the keyframes via JavaScript is a painful task, and changing the values of properties found inside any individual keyframe is even more painful.* Outside of a few generic properties, CSS animations were never designed to be dynamically changed once the animation has started running. They are a bit boring that way.

To contrast the boringness of CSS animations, we have CSS transitions. Because of how CSS transitions react to property changes anywhere on the element or elements they are listening for changes on, they are a great fit for dealing with changes provoked by Java-Script. For this reason, don't be surprised if almost all of the animations we modify with JavaScript rely on a CSS transition somewhere to make everything work.

Animating with requestAnimationFrame

There will be situations when you need to fully animate an element's CSS properties using JavaScript without relying on CSS transitions or animations. These aren't situations where you toggle some class values on an element or change a style property once in a blue moon. This is where you are running some JavaScript that needs to animate things on your page at a cool 60 fps without skipping a beat. All of this animation-related JavaScript is typically housed or triggered from a function commonly known as an *animation loop*.

Ensuring our animation loop runs smoothly depends on a lot of factors. It depends on what else is going on in your page, like what other animations might be running in parallel; how the user is interacting with the page (clicking, typing, scrolling, etc.); and what browser you are using and when it decides to repaint or update what is shown on the screen. It's not a simple problem.

Traditionally, you may have used a function like `setInterval` or its funnier cousin `setTimeOut` to power your animation loop. The problem with these two functions is simple: they don't understand the subtleties of working with the browser and getting things to paint at the right time. They have no awareness of what is going on in the rest of the page. These qualities made them very inefficient when it came to powering animations because they often request a repaint/update that your browser simply isn't ready to do. You would often end up with skipped frames and other horrible side effects.

Fortunately, we have something better! I'd like you to meet `requestA nimationFrame`. What makes `requestAnimationFrame` so awesome is that it doesn't force the browser to do a repaint that may never happen. Instead, it asks the browser nicely to call your animation loop when the browser decides it is time to redraw the screen. This means your code wastes no effort on screen updates that never happen. Skipped frames are a thing of the past. Best of all, because `requestAnimationFrame` is designed for animations, your browser optimizes the performance to ensure your animations run smoothly depending on how many system resources you have available, whether you are running on battery or not, whether you switch away to a different tab, and so on.

Words haven't been invented in the English language to describe how awesome the `requestAnimationFrame` function is. The way you use `requestAnimationFrame` is very simple. Whenever you want to redraw your screen, simply call it along with the name of the animation loop function (aka a callback) that is responsible for drawing stuff to your screen:

```
requestAnimationFrame(callback);
```

Note that the requestAnimationFrame function isn't a loop. It isn't a timer. You need to call it every time you want to get the screen repainted. This means, unless you want your animation to stop, you need to call requestAnimationFrame again through the same callback function that you specified. I know that sounds bizarre, but it looks as follows:

```
function animate() {

    // stuff for animating goes here

    requestAnimationFrame(animate);
}
requestAnimationFrame(animate);
```

The animate function is the callback function for our requestAnimationFrame call, and it will get called every time the browser needs to redraw once it starts running.

If this is your first time seeing the requestAnimationFrame function, its purpose may still seem a little mysterious. Don't worry. We will be looking at a handful of examples later on that owe everything to requestAnimationFrame's really performant way of repeatedly calling some code.

Conclusion

To create the kind of animated interactions your users will see when they interact with your UIs, you can't get away with just using CSS. You need to add JavaScript into the mix. As you saw in this chapter, that's not as scary as it sounds. In future chapters, we'll look at some practical examples that will really help you see the many ways CSS and JavaScript can play nicely together to help us create awesome animations.

CHAPTER 7

CSS Animations Versus CSS Transitions

As you've seen, right now in CSS you have two techniques for visualizing change that are competing for your attention: *CSS animations* and *CSS transitions*. On the surface, they seem similar. But once you get to know them, sort of like identical twins, you'll find that they are quite different in many important ways. In this chapter, we'll explore the similarities and the differences that exist between animations and transitions.

Almost everything you will see here will be a review of the core concepts the previous chapters introduced, but hopefully seeing them in the context of comparing animations and transitions will give you a different perspective on what you learned. Besides, the more you see animations and transitions defined and described, the more fluent you will be in thinking about them and knowing what to do.

Similarities

As I just mentioned, animations and transitions seem very similar—especially from a distance. They both allow you to:

- Specify which CSS properties to listen for changes on
- Set timing (easing) functions to alter the rate of going from a one property value to another
- Specify a duration to control how long the animation or transition will take

- Programmatically listen to animation and transition-specific events that you can then do with as you wish
- Visualize CSS property changes

Beyond these points, though, you will see that animations and transitions diverge a bit and let their uniqueness shine through. Let's look at those unique qualities in greater detail…and possibly pit them against each other in the playground for being different.

Differences

Animations and transitions show their differences when it comes to how you trigger them to play, whether they loop easily, how complicated of a transition you can define, how formal you must be in being able to use them, and how well they play with JavaScript. Let's explore those topics in greater detail.

Triggering

One of the major differences between animations and transitions is in how you trigger them to start playing.

A transition only plays as a reaction to a CSS property value that has changed. It doesn't care *how* a CSS property value was changed. As long as the computed value is different than what it recognizes, the transition starts firing.

For example, a common scenario is using the :hover pseudoclass to change the value of a CSS property (see Figure 7-1).

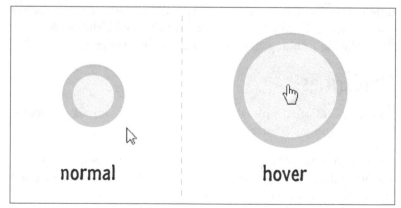

normal   **hover**

Figure 7-1. A common situation

The CSS for this could look as follows:

```css
.circle {
  border-radius: 100px;
  background-color: #DDF0FF;
  border: 10px solid #00CC00;
}
.circle:hover {
  transform: scale(2, 2);
}
```

By defining a transition that listens for a transform change, you could see the circle growing from its normal size:

```css
.circle {
  border-radius: 100px;
  background-color: #DDF0FF;
  border: 10px solid #00CC00;
  transition: transform .2s ease-out;
}
.circle:hover {
  transform: scale(2, 2);
}
```

Another way of triggering a transition is to use JavaScript to programmatically add or remove CSS classes to simulate a CSS property value change. As long as the computed value of a property the transition is listening for changes, the transition will become active.

Rounding out our ways of making a property change, you can use JavaScript to set an inline style that changes a property your transition is listening for. To make our circle's size change on click, your code might look as follows:

```javascript
var circle = document.querySelector(".circle");
circle.addEventListener("click", changeSize, false);

function changeSize(e) {
  circle.style.transform = "scale(4, 4)";
}
```

The highlighted line is the most interesting one. Even though I am setting the transform property via JavaScript, because our transition has already been defined in CSS, this change will get animated. This ability for transitions to be triggered by changes in code is *one of the coolest things ever*, and you'll see us take advantage of it in later tutorials when we do more advanced things.

Animations, on the other hand, don't require any explicit triggering. Once you define the animation, it will start playing automatically.

You can control this behavior by setting the `animation-play-state` property to `running` or `paused`.

Looping

This is pretty simple. We can easily make animations loop by setting the `animation-iteration-count` property. You can specify a fixed number of times you want your animation to repeat:

```
animation-iteration-count: 5;
```

If you just want your animation to loop forever, you can do that as well:

```
animation-iteration-count: infinite;
```

Transitions, on the other hand, don't have a property that specifies how many times they can run. When triggered, a transition runs only once. You can make a transition loop by fiddling with the `transitionEnd` event, but that isn't particularly straightforward—especially when compared with how easy it is to make animations loop. We won't be looking at that event in this book, but you can find more about it in my post "The TransitionEnd Event" (*https://www.kirupa.com/html5/the_transitionend_event.htm*).

Defining Intermediate Points/Keyframes

As you've seen, with an animation, you have the ability to define keyframes that give you more control over your CSS property values beyond just the start and the end (Figure 7-2).

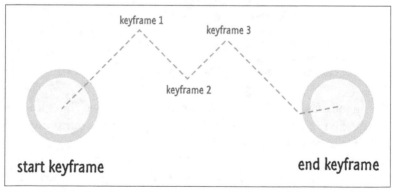

Figure 7-2. Animations allow you to specify intermediate points where anything could happen!

You can set as many keyframes as you want, and when your animation plays, each keyframe will be hit with the specified property changes reflected. Each keyframe can even have its own timing function, so you can make the interpolation between the CSS property values defined between keyframes really interesting if you want!

With a transition, you don't have much control over anything beyond the end result (Figure 7-3).

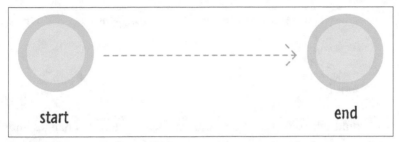

Figure 7-3. Transitions go from point A to point B...that's it!

A transition simply goes from an initial state to the final state. You cannot specify any points in between like you can with an animation, so a transition might not be a good choice for anything remotely complex.

Specifying Properties Up Front

Next, we'll go over the difference in formality between animations and transitions when it comes to defining a transition between CSS property values.

As expected, on the formal side, you have transitions. Every CSS property you want recognized by your transition must be explicitly represented.

For example, let's say you have some CSS that looks like the following:

```
#mainContent {
  background-color: #CC0000;
  transition: background-color .5s ease-in;
}
#mainContent:hover {
  cursor: pointer;
  background-color: #000000;
  width: 500px;
}
```

Upon hover, we specify a different value for background-color as well as width. Our transition is listening only for changes on background-color, though. If we want our transition to react to changes in both the background-color and width properties, we will need to explicitly add another transition entry for the width property:

```
#mainContent {
    background-color: #CC0000;
    transition: background-color .5s ease-in, width .5s ease-in;
}
#mainContent:hover {
    cursor: pointer;
    background-color: #000000;
    width: 500px;
}
```

You could tell your transition to listen for all property changes and specify the all keyword, but for performance reasons, you shouldn't default to it. Of course, as with all claims about performance benefits or pitfalls, you should see if it is applicable to your scenario before taking my word for it.

With animations, you can specify properties on a whim in each keyframe without having to do anything that even closely resembles declaring them:

```
@keyframes imageSlide {
    0% {
        transform: translate(-150px, 0);
    }
    20% {
        transform: translate(50px, 0)
        height: 200px;
    }
    80% {
        transform: translate(200px, 0)
        height: 300px;
    }
    100% {
        transform: translate(600px, 0)
        background-color: #FFFFFF;
    }
}
```

In this example, the height and background-color properties of whatever element we're animating will smoothly transition—even if the property was never listed before!

Interaction with JavaScript

Long and Boring Block of Text Ahead

TL;DR: if you want to manipulate how something animates using JavaScript, just use a CSS transition. CSS animations are no fun in this area because of how complex it is to access and manipulate them using code.

In some cases, a transition or animation you declare in CSS will be good enough. You specify in CSS your starting value, the ending value, and any intermediate values that you want your properties to take. Your animation or transition will read these values and take care of business from there. As we saw earlier with our random color example, sometimes you will need to change the final property value on the fly. For such situations, you will need something like JavaScript.

When it comes to combining JavaScript with either an animation or transition, there is no contest: you almost always want to use a transition. Using an animation with JavaScript is possible...in much the same way it is possible to win at the cinnamon challenge (*http:// bit.ly/mbCinnamonChallenge*). It isn't impossible to make it work, but chances are, you don't want to do it. The reason for this difference has to do with how transitions and animations work.

Animations are very specific in what they do. The reason is that the @keyframes rule clearly lays out the path your animation will take as it is running. Every property value that will get affected is defined in your keyframes. There is no room for interpretation or alteration. Attempting to change your keyframes in JavaScript requires a very complicated series of steps that involves actually modifying the @keyframes style rule itself. If you've ever had to manipulate CSS that lives inside a style rule, you know that it is pretty unintuitive. If you've never done that before, it is definitely worth trying at least once...and only once.

In contrast to the predefined path of an animation is the transition. Transitions are not as well defined as they may seem. Your transition will kick in when a property it is listening for changes. As you saw earlier, the transition doesn't care how the properties it is listening for changes. As long as the property changes somehow, the transition will get to work. This means that for interactive scenarios that don't involve a predefined starting and ending point, you can do a lot of interesting things by deferring all transition-related heavy lifting by setting the transition property in CSS and manipulating all of the values the transition is listening for using JavaScript. We'll be seeing a lot of this in the future.

Conclusion

Now that you have a good idea of the full range of what animations and transitions can do, you probably already have your thoughts on when you would use one over the other.

My general approach for determining when to use which goes like this:

- If what I want requires the flexibility provided by having multiple keyframes, then I go with an animation.
- If I am looking for a simple from/to animation, then I go with a transition.
- If I want my animation to start automatically or loop, then I go with an animation.
- If I want to manipulate the property values that I wish to animate using JavaScript, I go with a transition.

Now, with enough effort and JavaScript tomfoolery, you can neutralize any of the differences listed in deciding whether to use a transition or an animation. My recommendations are based on the common cases where you take a transition or animation mostly at face value. Herculean efforts to change their default behavior are admirable but often unnecessary.

PART II
Learning from Examples

This is probably the part of the book you have been waiting for. Or dreading. This is the part where we take everything we've learned in the previous seven chapters and apply it toward creating the types of animations you see used throughout our user interfaces. Yes, this does mean that we'll be seeing less of happily smiling geometric shapes and more of the traditional buttons, scroll bars, links, and other widgets that everybody sees, clicks, types, or taps on every day.

We'll start off with some simple examples before we slowly start turning up the complexity and looking at examples that push the boundaries on what we can do using HTML, CSS, and JavaScript.

Enjoy!

CHAPTER 8

Animating Your Links to Life

Back in the day, links were very predefined and boring. They were made up of underlined blue text that turned purple if you had already visited them. Often, there was also a mysterious active state where your links would turn red when you were interacting with them. They looked sorta like the following:

how links looked in the 1800s

Today, you have a lot more control to make your links look as boring or as exciting as you want. Since we are all about doing exciting things, this tutorial will show you a handful of examples that you can learn from to make your links behave differently (in an awesome way!) when you interact with them. *Spoiler alert:* The main way we are going to do that is by relying on our old friend, the CSS transition.

The Starting Point

To help you focus on what is important, let's start with some HTML that contains some basic styling and links. In a new HTML document, add all of the following:

```html
<!DOCTYPE html>
<html>

<head>
  <title>Cool Hover Stuff!!!</title>
  <style>
    body {
      background-color: #EEE;
      margin: 50px;
    }
    h1, li {
      font-family: sans-serif;
    }
    h1 {
      background-color: #FFCC00;
      display: inline-block;
      padding: 10px;
    }
    li {
      margin-bottom: 30px;
      font-size: 24px;
    }
  </style>
</head>

<body>
  <h1>Halloween Ideas</h1>
  <ul>
    <li><a href="#" target="_blank">
      Copernicus</a></li>
    <li><a href="#" target="_blank">
      Yoda</a></li>
    <li><a href="#" target="_blank">
      Mega Man</a></li>
    <li><a href="#" target="_blank">
      Gandalf</a></li>
    <li><a href="#" target="_blank">
      Bono</a></li>
  </ul>
</body>

</html>
```

Once you've added all of this, save your document and preview it in the browser. If everything worked out properly, you'll see something that looks like this:

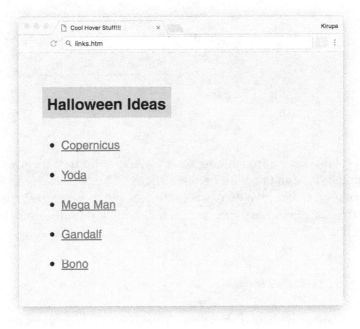

If you see this, you are in good shape. There is nothing crazy going on in this page, but take a few moments to look at the markup and double-check to ensure nothing seems out of place. In the following sections we'll extend this example by figuring out how to make our boring blue and underlined links do some cool stuff when you hover over them with your mouse.

Animated Underline

The first effect we are going to look at is a pretty simple one: underlining the links when you hover over them. This underline won't just suddenly appear. It will be something we animate in:

Awesome Link $\longrightarrow$ Awesome Link

Awesome Link

Awesome Link

Awesome Link

NORMAL   *HOVER*

Let's slowly walk through how we are going to do this. Right now, our links have an underline on them already. They also appear in the default blue color. We don't want either of those things. Inside the `style` block in our markup, add the following style rule toward the bottom:

```
li a {
  color: #0066FF;
  text-decoration: none;
}
```

All we are doing here is changing our link color to a different shade of blue, and we are setting the `text-decoration` property to `none` to hide the underline. If you preview this change in your browser, our links will appear with a nicer shade of blue and without any underline. This is good for our initial link state.

When we hover over a link, we want it to get underlined. One very reasonable solution might be to add a style rule that looks something like the following:

```
li a:hover {
  text-decoration: underline;
}
```

When we hover over our link, we set the `text-decoration` property to `underline`—after we used the `text-decoration` property to hide the underline earlier! Next, because we would like this change to be animated, we can throw in a transition by declaring it in our `li a` style rule:

```
li a {
  color: #0066FF;
  text-decoration: none;
  transition: all .2s ease-out;
}
```

Go ahead and make these changes, preview in your browser, and hover over any of the links. You will see that your links underline when you hover over them, but you won't see the underlines getting animated. They just suddenly appear. What is going on?

This behavior has to do with an important detail about animating CSS properties: *not all CSS properties can be animated.* MDN maintains a pretty comprehensive list (*https://developer.mozilla.org/en-US/docs/Web/CSS/CSS_animated_properties*) of properties that can be animated, and the `text-decoration` property isn't listed. So, we need to find an alternate underlining solution involving a CSS property whose values can be animated easily.

That magical CSS property is `border`. This property is traditionally used to add a border around the bounding box of an element. We'll specify a border to appear only on the bottom of an element. To do this, modify the `li a:hover` style rule with the following:

```
li a:hover {
  border-bottom: 4px solid #0066FF;
}
```

What we are doing here is setting the `border-bottom` shorthand property. This results in us getting the equivalent of an underline that is 4 pixels thick. If you preview this change in your browser, you'll see our border gradually animate in when you hover over any of the links with your mouse. But we aren't done with this effect just yet.

Note that the property getting animated isn't fully the `border-bottom` property. It is the `border-bottom-width` property, which our shorthand declaration maps to, where we go from a border width of 0px to a border width of 4px. This is why our animation shows the border actually increasing in size when you hover over the link as opposed to it just gradually appearing. If you like the border growing effect, that's great! If you want something more traditional, such as having the underline fade in without increasing in size (sort of like what we set out to do), we can choose to animate another border-related property such as the color:

```
li a {
  color: #0066FF;
  text-decoration: none;
  transition: all .2s ease-out;
  border-bottom: 4px solid rgba(0, 102, 255, 0);
}
li a:hover {
  border-bottom: 4px solid rgba(0, 102, 255, 1);
}
```

In this version, we are specifying our underline's blue color as an RGBA value with the last value being the alpha or transparency. A value of 0 means the color is fully transparent. A value of 1 means the color is fully visible. By change the alpha value between the normal and hover states, we ensure our transition animates the underline color by fading in and out as expected. Yay!

Listening for All Property Changes

You may have noticed that our transition declaration is listening for changes on *all* properties:

```
transition: all .2s ease-out;
```

For performance-related reasons, I may have mentioned that you should specify the exact property you are listening for instead of using the more convenient *all*. For situations like this, the performance implication will be minor.

Simple Background Color Change

The next effect we'll look at is changing our link's background color when we hover over it. There are two variations of this that we will look at, but we'll start with the easy one where we simply animate the link's background color.

This effect can be visualized as follows:

Awesome Link $\longrightarrow$ Awesome Link

Awesome Link

Awesome Link

Awesome Link

NORMAL *HOVER*

We add this behavior by setting the `background-color` property to the color we want when you hover over the link. Go ahead and modify your existing `li a` and `li a:hover` style rules to look like this:

```
li a {
  color: #0066FF;
  text-decoration: none;
  transition: all .2s ease-out;
  padding: 3px;
}
li a:hover {
  background-color: #B5E1FF;
}
```

The changes aren't big—even if you were just replacing some existing markup from our underline effect earlier. We increased our transition duration to .2s, added a `padding` value of 3px to ensure we give our background color some breathing room, and we set the `background-color` property to #B5E1FF when you hover over a link. If you preview all of these changes in the browser, you'll see our links get a light blue background when you hover over them. Pretty straightforward, right?

Cooler Background Color Change

Now, let's do something a little more exciting. Instead of the background color just fading into view, let's have it actually slide into view. This effect would look something like this:

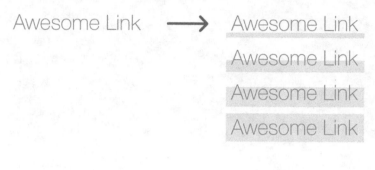

NORMAL

HOVER

This effect is a little more involved than what we've seen so far, because it requires you to (literally) think outside the box a bit. This effect is made up of a linear gradient where half of the background is transparent, and the other half is the blue color that we want:

transparent →

transparent → Awesome Link *← blue*

← blue

Obviously, we don't quite want our link to look like this. We don't want any color to be seen initially, and the color is only visible when we hover over the link. The way we get what we want is by scaling the background to twice its height:

What you see! Awesome Link *Double the gradient height!*

This allows only the transparent portion to be visible by default. The blue colored region is hidden away just below where our link is. When we hover over the link, we slide the gradient up—animating the bottom half of the gradient that is hidden from view until it takes up the full height of our link.

You've seen a lot of words so far to describe this effect. It's time to look at the implementation. Go back to your markup and change your li a and li a:hover style rules to the following:

```
li a {
  color: #0066FF;
  text-decoration: none;
  transition: all .2s ease-out;
  padding: 3px;
  background: linear-gradient(to bottom,
                  rgba(181, 225, 255, 0) 0%,
                  rgba(181, 225, 255, 0) 50%,
                  rgba(181, 225, 255, 1) 50%,
                  rgba(181, 225, 255, 1) 100%);
  background-repeat: no-repeat;
  background-size: 100% 200%;
}
li a:hover {
  background-position: 0 100%;
}
```

Take a few moments to walk through the markup and see how it relates to the explanation in the previous paragraphs. Then preview these changes in your browser to make sure everything works fine. Once you've done that, let's look at the code in a little more detail.

Some of the code highlights include us specifying the linear gradient by setting the linear-gradient function to the background property:

```
background: linear-gradient(to bottom,
                rgba(181, 225, 255, 0) 0%,
                rgba(181, 225, 255, 0) 50%,
                rgba(181, 225, 255, 1) 50%,
                rgba(181, 225, 255, 1) 100%);
```

We double the gradient's height by relying on the background-size property:

```
background-size: 100% 200%;
```

With our gradient defined and doubled in size, our links won't look special at all when you look at them initially. When you hover over them, that changes thanks to the following:

```
li a:hover {
  background-position: 0 100%;
}
```

We shift our background's position vertically by 100% when our `li a:hover` selector becomes active. The 100% here does not refer to the height of our background. It refers to the bounding box of the link element (aka the `a` element), so that's why shifting by 100% doesn't shift our gradient completely out of view.

Conclusion

Links are everywhere in almost everything you will be creating. By providing some sort of animated feedback when a user hovers over them, you've utilized animations in a very subtle and meaningful way. Subtle and meaningful aren't bad things to be associated with animations, so that's...um...a good thing! Getting more into the technical side, the examples we've seen all involved the `transition` property. Transitions are great because you are often changing a handful of properties upon hovering that you'd like to animate. You get the animation for free basically. This doesn't mean that you can't use CSS animations for hover effects, though. You can certainly create more elaborate effects using keyframes and the `animation` property, so give that a shot if you are up for creating some cooler hover effects than what we've seen here!

CHAPTER 9

Simple Text Fade and Scale Animation

Not all animations have to be flashy and doing all sorts of things to grab your attention. Some of the best uses for animation are in the subtle cases—the cases where you may not even notice an animation is present. In this chapter, we'll create one such animation whose existence is purely to add some sugary, frosty value. To see this animation, navigate your browser to *http://bit.ly/subtle_animation*.

If you don't have access to a browser where you can view it live, Figure 9-1 shows what our example looks like once it has fully animated into view.

Figure 9-1. The boring, static version of our example

This example is a very quick animation that fades some text in. Along with the fade, your text scales (or zooms) in as well. In this deconstruction, we'll look at how this effect was created by primarily focusing on the CSS animation responsible for it.

The Example

The full HTML and CSS for this example looks as follows:

```html
<!DOCTYPE html>
<html>

<head>
  <title>Example Of Many Things!</title>
  <style>
    body {
      background-color: #F5F5F5;
      margin: 50px;
      margin: 25px 0 0 0;
    }
    #main {
      text-align: center;
      background-color: #82C1FF;
      width: 600px;
      height: 300px;
      margin: 0 auto;
      border-radius: 5px;
    }
    h1 {
      font-size: 88px;
      font-family: Arial, Helvetica, sans-serif;
      font-weight: normal;
      color: #FFF;
      margin: 0;
      padding: 90px 0 25px 0;
      transform-origin: 50% 100%;
      text-shadow: 2px 2px 2px #333;

      animation-duration: .3s;
      animation-name: fadeAndScale;
      animation-timing-function: cubic-bezier(.71,.55,.62,1.57);
    }
    a {
      font-family: Cambria, Cochin, serif;
      font-size: 16px;
      color: #333;
      padding: 5px;
      border-radius: 5px;
      background-color: #A6D2FF;
      transition: background-color .2s ease-out;
```

```
    }
    a:hover {
        background-color: #EEE;
    }
    @keyframes fadeAndScale {
        from {
            opacity: 0;
            transform: scale(.9, .9);
        }
        to {
            opacity: 1;
            transform: scale(1, 1);
        }
    }
    </style>
</head>

<body>
    <div id="main">
        <h1>hi, everybody!</h1>
        <p><a href="#"
                onclick="window.location.reload(true);return false;">
            reload
        </a>
        </p>
    </div>
</body>

</html>
```

Take a few moments and try to see how this markup maps to the animation linked to earlier. After you've done that, let's walk through the interesting parts of this example together.

The CSS Animation

Nothing is more important in this example than the animation! As you can see, the fade and scale animation affects the "hi, everybody!" text. That text is represented by an h1 tag in our HTML:

```
<h1>hi, everybody!</h1>
```

The look of this h1 tag is modified by the generic h1 style rule that lives in your CSS:

```
h1 {
    font-size: 88px;
    font-family: Arial, Helvetica, sans-serif;
    font-weight: normal;
    color: #FFF;
```

```
    margin: 0;
    padding: 90px 0 25px 0;
    transform-origin: 50% 100%;
    text-shadow: 2px 2px 2px #333;

    animation-duration: .3s;
    animation-name: fadeAndScale;
    animation-timing-function: cubic-bezier(.71,.55,.62,1.57);
}
```

Besides just specifying the look, this style rule contains your animation declaration as well:

```
h1 {
    .

    .

    .
    animation-duration: .3s;
    animation-name: fadeAndScale;
    animation-timing-function: cubic-bezier(.71,.55,.62,1.57);
}
```

The highlighted lines make up our animation declaration. This should be pretty straightforward. Our animation is set to run a spritely .3 seconds, the name of our @keyframes rule where the actual animation details live is fadeAndScale, and we're using a custom easing function to alter how our animation runs. More on the easing function a bit later, but let's look at our fadeAndScale @keyframes next:

```
@keyframes fadeAndScale {
  from {
    opacity: 0;
    transform: scale(.9, .9);
  }
  to {
    opacity: 1;
    transform: scale(1, 1);
  }
}
```

In case you didn't notice, the real action for any CSS animation always lives in the keyframes. Our case is no different. Because our animation is essentially a transition between a start and ending state, we have just a from and to keyframe where our animation's behavior is defined.

The from keyframe defines the starting state of the animation:

```
@keyframes fadeAndScale {
  from {
    opacity: 0;
    transform: scale(.9, .9);
  }
  to {
    opacity: 1;
    transform: scale(1, 1);
  }
}
```

From looking at our animation, we can tell that our text starts off invisible and is smaller than it needs to be. The contents of this keyframe formally define our observation where the opacity is set to 0 and the scale function is set to .9, or 90%.

The to keyframe defines what happens in the end:

```
@keyframes fadeAndScale {
  from {
    opacity: 0;
    transform: scale(.9, .9);
  }
  to {
    opacity: 1;
    transform: scale(1, 1);
  }
}
```

Mapping to what we visually observe, in the end state, our text is fully visible and its scale is set to 1, or 100%. That's all there is to it.

Everything you see in our keyframes should match what you see in the actual example. In the actual example, our text does in fact fade in. It also scales up a little bit. All of that was defined by our from and to keyframes with some extra input from the animation declaration where the duration and easing function were specified. Putting all of that together, you get the animation that you see. Now, speaking of the easing function...

The Easing Function

There is another subtle effect inside our already subtle animation (*Inception* style!) that I want to point out. If you pay close attention to how our text fades and scales in, you'll notice that there is a slight bounce at the end where our text grows a bit larger than it needs to and then snaps back into place.

Figure 9-2 describes this effect.

Figure 9-2. We overshoot the text size and then snap it back

This is made possible thanks to our custom easing function:

```
animation-timing-function: cubic-bezier(.71,.55,.62,1.57);
```

You can visualize this easing function on the cubic-bezier genera-tor site (*http://cubic-bezier.com/#.71,.55,.62,1.57*) we talked about in Chapter 4:

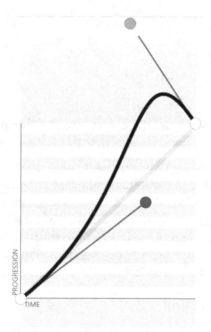

From visualizing our cubic-bezier points, the effect you see should make more sense. Even though your keyframes defined a clear start-ing and ending value for our opacity property and scale function, the easing function controls the property values in between...often in interesting ways that go beyond the strictly defined boundaries set at the beginning and end of an animation.

Conclusion

The goal of this example was to simply provide you with another look at how the animation and keyframe syntax work together. Despite the noble goals of keeping this example simple, the easing function definitely adds a certain level of flair. Remember, no matter how simple your animation is, you should always strive to make it as lifelike as possible. Overshooting your target and snapping back into position, as accomplished by our easing function, is a classic animation technique that represents how things move in real life. With very little added effort on our part, our custom easing function made this animation even cooler than it originally was!

CHAPTER 10

Creating a Smooth Sliding Menu

In UIs today, sliding menus are all the rage. These menus are basically off-screen elements that slide into view when you click or tap on an arrow, a hamburger icon, or something else that indicates a menu will appear.

To see a sliding menu like this in action, visit *https://www.kirupa.com/html5/examples/slidingmenu.htm*.

If you aren't able to view this menu live, let's re-create it statically. At first, you'll have your page:

What you see initially!

There will be some UI that you will interact with to bring up the menu. In our case, that is the blue circle you see in the top-left corner. When you click on it, the menu will smoothly slide into view:

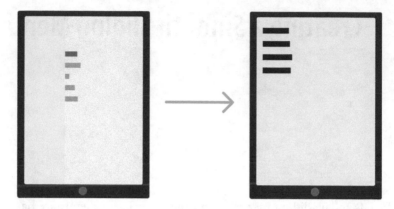

When you click anywhere on the menu, the menu will smoothly slide back and disappear, and your original page content will be visible again. In this chapter, you'll learn all about how to create a menu like this.

How the Sliding Menu Works

Before we jump into the code, let's take a few moments to better understand how exactly our sliding menu works. As it turns out, this menu relies on some simple layout and positioning tricks. See, the menu is never truly nonexistent. It is simply hidden outside of view.

To see what that looks like, take a look at the following image:

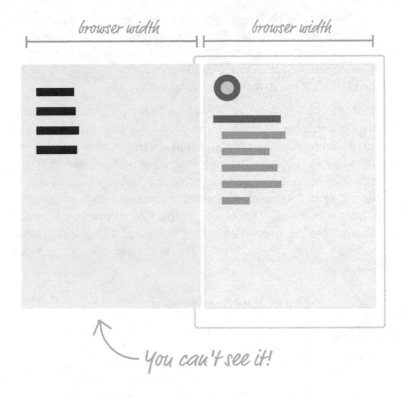

browser width   _browser width_

You can't see it!

Just to the left of the content that we see, we have our menu... patiently hiding until it is called upon. We implement that behavior by shifting the menu as far left as we can until it is fully out of view. Figuring out how far to shift is easy. Our menu's size is the same as our browser's window (aka the viewport) size, because we want the menu to fully cover up whatever is shown. Given that detail, we just shift the menu left by the browser's width. One way of doing that is by using the following CSS:

```
#theMenu {
    position: fixed;
    left: 0;
    top: 0;
    transform: translate3d(-100vw, 0, 0);

    width: 100vw;
    height: 100vh;
}
```

We set our menu's `position` to `fixed`. This single change gives our menu a whole lot of magical capabilities. For starters, this ensures normal layout rules no longer apply to it. We can position our menu anywhere we want using normal *x* and *y* values, and the menu won't shift away from where we have it positioned. And as if all of that isn't awesome enough, our menu won't even display a scroll bar if we happen to hide it somewhere offscreen.

All of this is a good thing, as the way we hide our menu offscreen is by setting our menu's `left` and `top` properties to 0 and setting our menu's `transform` property to a `translate3d` function with a horizontal value of `-100vw`. The negative value ensures we shift the menu left by an amount equivalent to our browser window's width. While not related to position directly, the size of our menu plays an important role as well. That is why in this CSS snippet, we have the `width` and `height` properties set to values of `100vw` and `100vh`, respectively, to ensure our menu's size is the same as our browser window's size.

What Are These vw and vh Units?

If you've never seen the `vw` and `vh` units before, they stand for *viewport width* (`vw`) and *viewport height* (`vh`). They are a bit similar to percentage values. Each unit is 1/100 the width or height of your viewport (what we've been simply calling the browser window). For example, a value of `100vw` represents the full width of our browser window. Similarly, `100vh` refers to a value that is the full height of our browser window.

When the menu is called upon to slide into view, we slide the menu right until its horizontal position is the same as our browser window origin. The CSS for it would be an easy change from what we already have. We simply set our `transform` property's `translate3d` function and set the horizontal position to a value of `0vw`.

This might look something like this:

```
#theMenu.visible {
    transform: translate3d(0vw, 0, 0);
}
```

This change ensures our menu is shifted right from being hidden offscreen (with a horizontal translate value of `-100vw`) and is now visible.

The only thing we haven't covered is the animation that makes the sliding look cool. The reason we haven't covered it yet is because this is the easy part! The sliding is accomplished with a CSS transition that animates the changes to our `transform` property's `translate3d` function that we make to toggle our menu from being off- or on-screen:

```
transition: transform .3s cubic-bezier(0, .52, 0, 1);
```

That's it. What we've done in this section is take a bird's-eye view of how our sliding menu works. There are a few details that we haven't looked at, but we'll address them next as part of actually building this menu.

Creating the Sliding Menu

Now that you have a really good idea about how our sliding menu works, let's turn all of that theoretical knowledge into some sweet markup and code.

The Initial Page

The first part of this involves just getting our example off the ground. This is the boring part where we create the initial page with some boilerplate content, but we have to do it...just like eating vegetables.

Create a new HTML document and add the following content into it:

```html
<!DOCTYPE html>
<html>

<head>
  <meta name="viewport"
        content="width=device-width, initial-scale=1.0" />
  <title>Sliding Menu</title>

  <style>
    body {
      background-color: #EEE;
      font-family: Helvetica, Arial, sans-serif;
      padding: 25px;
      margin: 0;
      overflow: auto;
    }
```

```
      #container li {
        margin-bottom: 10px;
      }

      #roundButton {
        background-color: #96D9FF;
        margin-bottom: 20px;
        width: 50px;
        height: 50px;
        border-radius: 50%;
        border: 10px solid #0065A6;
        outline: none;
        transition: transform .3s cubic-bezier(0, .52, 0, 1);
      }

      #roundButton:hover {
        background-color: #96D9FF;
        cursor: pointer;
        border-color: #003557;
        transform: scale(1.2, 1.2);
      }

      #roundButton:active {
        border-color: #003557;
        background-color: #FFF;
      }
    </style>
  </head>

<body>
  <button id="roundButton"></button>
  <div id="container">
    <p>Can you spot the item that doesn't belong?</p>
    <ul>
      <li>Lorem</li>
      <li>Ipsum</li>
      <li>Dolor</li>
      <li>Sit</li>
      <li>Bumblebees</li>
      <li>Aenean</li>
      <li>Consectetur</li>
    </ul>
  </div>

  <script>

  </script>
</body>

</html>
```

After you've added all of this content, save your document and preview it in your browser to make sure everything loads and looks correct. You should see something that looks as follows:

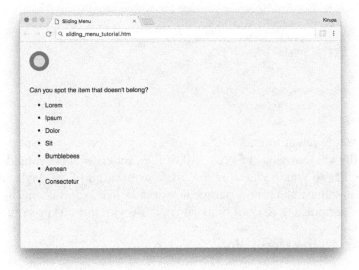

Clicking on the blue button won't do anything, but that's OK for now. We'll fix that in a few moments.

Adding the Menu

Now that our initial page has been created, we are going to add the menu. In our HTML just below the body tag, add the following:

```html
<div id="flyoutMenu">
    <h2><a href="#">Home</a></h2>
    <h2><a href="#">About</a></h2>
    <h2><a href="#">Contact</a></h2>
    <h2><a href="#">Search</a></h2>
</div>
```

Once you've done this, we need to add the corresponding CSS as well. In your style region, add the following style rules:

```css
#flyoutMenu {
    width: 100vw;
    height: 100vh;
    background-color: #FFE600;
    position: fixed;
    top: 0;
```

```
  left: 0;
  transform: translate3d(-100vw, 0, 0);
  transition: transform .3s cubic-bezier(0, .52, 0, 1);
}

#flyoutMenu h2 a {
  color: #333;
  margin-left: 15px;
  text-decoration: none;
}

#flyoutMenu h2 a:hover {
  text-decoration: underline;
}
```

Take a moment to understand what each property does—especially in the #flyoutMenu style rule. All of the properties there should be familiar to you, because we looked at a variation of this style rule when talking about how our menu works earlier. We will come back to it periodically, so don't think you're done with this one just yet!

Making the Menu Work

The last (and probably most important) step is to make our menu actually slide in and slide out. We do this by using a combination of JavaScript and CSS. The CSS part is the easy one, so let's look at that first. In your style region, add the following style rule:

```
#flyoutMenu.show {
  transform: translate3d(0vw, 0, 0);
}
```

This .show style rule sets the horizontal position to 0vw, and it is attached to our #flyoutMenu style rule to ensure we overwrite the value it originally had. Now, moving away from the CSS…

Inside our script tags, add the following:

```
var roundButton = document.querySelector("#roundButton");
roundButton.addEventListener("click", showMenu, false);

var flyoutMenu = document.querySelector("#flyoutMenu");
flyoutMenu.addEventListener("click", hideMenu, false);

function showMenu(e) {
  flyoutMenu.classList.add("show");

}

function hideMenu(e) {
```

```
flyoutMenu.classList.remove("show");
e.stopPropagation();

}
```

What these lines of code do is pretty simple…on the surface. They ensure our menu appears when we click on the blue circular button, and they ensure our menu disappears when we click anywhere inside the menu. Let's look at these lines of code in greater detail.

Listening to events

The first four lines just deal with referencing the DOM elements in JavaScript and setting up the event listeners that will help us listen and react to the click event:

```
var roundButton = document.querySelector("#roundButton");
roundButton.addEventListener("click", showMenu, true);

var flyoutMenu = document.querySelector("#flyoutMenu");
flyoutMenu.addEventListener("click", hideMenu, false);
```

Referencing the DOM elements for our blue circular button and the menu is straightforward. We use the querySelector method to help us find these elements, our blue circular button is referenced via the roundButton variable, and our menu is referenced by the flyout Menu variable.

Once we have a reference to our button and menu, all that remains is to listen for click events on them. When our button (of circular and blue disposition!) is clicked, we will be calling the showMenu function. When our menu is clicked, we will be calling the hideMenu function. A lot of interesting things happen inside these two functions, so let's tackle them next.

Showing the menu

The showMenu function is responsible for getting our menu to appear:

```
function showMenu(e) {
  flyoutMenu.classList.add("show");
}
```

The only thing it does is dynamically add the show class value to our menu:

```
<div class="show" id="flyoutMenu">
  <h2><a href="#">Home</a></h2>
  <h2><a href="#">About</a></h2>
  <h2><a href="#">Contact</a></h2>
  <h2><a href="#">Search</a></h2>
</div>
```

The reason we do this is to allow the .show style rule we added ear-lier to become active on our menu element. If you recall, in our CSS, our menu's default horizontal position is -100vw:

```
#flyoutMenu {
  width: 100vw;
  height: 100vh;
  background-color: #FFE600;
  position: fixed;
  top: 0;
  left: 0;
  transform: translate3d(-100vw, 0, 0);
  transition: transform .3s cubic-bezier(0, .52, 0, 1);
}
```

After we get the .show style rule to apply on our menu, we set the new horizontal position to 0vw:

```
.show {
  transform: translate3d(0vw, 0, 0);
}
```

This is what ensures our menu goes from being hidden initially to now showing up. Because we have a transition listening for changes to the transform property in our #flyoutMenu style rule, this change in our horizontal translate value from -100vw to 0vw isn't sudden. It is animated!

You know what's even more crazy? All of what we just talked about happens when our one lonely line of JavaScript, which simply adds the show class value to our flyoutMenu element, gets run!

Hiding the menu

The code for hiding our menu looks like the following:

```
function hideMenu(e) {
    flyoutMenu.classList.remove("show");
    e.stopPropagation();
}
```

Here, we do the opposite of what we did in the showMenu function. We remove the show class value from our flyoutMenu element. This ensures our `.show` style no longer applies, and our menu's horizontal position is set back to its original translate value of `-100vw`.

There is one extra wrinkle in this function that we didn't have with `showMenu`, though. We call the `stopPropagation` method to prevent our `click` event from traveling beyond our menu's borders. We do this to safeguard other elements on the page that might also be listening to `click` events from accidentally reacting to our menu click.

Wait...What About Not Transmitting the Click Event?

If the `stopPropagation` method's behavior doesn't fully make sense, it has to do with how events are fired and travel up and down through our DOM. Explaining that fully goes beyond the boundaries of this chapter, but not to worry! Check out the Event Capturing and Bubbling tutorial (*http://bit.ly/2mFRj0S*), which covers the weird migration pattern of events in great detail. It will help you make sense of why stopping our event from traveling beyond our menu is a good idea.

Adding Some Finishing Touches

OK! If you preview your page right now, your menu should slide in and slide out exactly as you might expect. Now, this would be where we pat ourselves on the back for a job well done and move on to the next thing. As it turns out, our menu *looks* functional, but there are a handful of important usability details we need to add to ensure our menu is *actually* functional.

Dealing with scrolling

An annoying part of menus revolves around scrolling. When the menu is displayed, we don't want to scroll the page that is hidden behind the menu. The only thing that should scroll is the menu itself if it shows more content than can fit in one screen. Right now, the exact opposite happens. We can't scroll the menu, and the contents behind the menu scroll happily when the menu is displayed. Fixing this isn't too complicated, though.

The first thing we are going to do is enable scrolling on our menu when the content requires it. In our `#flyoutMenu` style rule, add the following highlighted line:

```css
#flyoutMenu {
    width: 100vw;
    height: 100vh;
    background-color: #FFE600;
    position: fixed;
    top: 0;
    left: 0;
    transform: translate3d(-100vw, 0, 0);
    transition: transform .3s cubic-bezier(0, .52, 0, 1);
    overflow: scroll;
}
```

By setting the `overflow` property to `scroll`, we tell our browser that it is OK to display scroll bars and allow out-of-view content in our menu to be scrolled into view.

The next thing we do is ensure the rest of our document can't be scrolled when the menu is displayed. The easiest way to accomplish this is by adding a small amount of JavaScript. Inside our `showMenu` and `hideMenu` functions, add the following two highlighted lines:

```javascript
function showMenu(e) {
    flyoutMenu.classList.add("show");

    document.body.style.overflow = "hidden";
}

function hideMenu(e) {
    flyoutMenu.classList.remove("show");
    e.stopPropagation();

    document.body.style.overflow = "auto";
}
```

Inside the `showMenu` function that gets called when our menu is about to display, we set the `overflow` property on our body element to `hidden`. This ensures you can't scroll the overall page when the menu is up. When the menu disappears, we want to restore regular scrolling. That is what we do in the `hideMenu` function when we set our body element's `overflow` property to `auto`.

Ensuring our menu appears above everything else

Just like dealing with stacks of paper, every element in your page has a vertical order in the stack known as the *z-index*. The z-index determines which elements are visible and which elements get covered up by other elements. We want to ensure our menu is the topmost element on the page and not covered up (even partially) by other elements on the page.

To ensure our desired topmost behavior, we set the `z-index` property in CSS. Inside our `#flyoutMenu` style rule, add the following highlighted line:

```
#flyoutMenu {
    width: 100vw;
    height: 100vh;
    background-color: #FFE600;
    position: fixed;
    top: 0;
    left: 0;
    transform: translate3d(-100vw, 0, 0);
    transition: transform .3s cubic-bezier(0, .52, 0, 1);
    overflow: scroll;
    z-index: 1000;
}
```

We added the `z-index` property and gave it a value of `1000`. The higher the value of our `z-index` property, the higher up in our stack of HTML elements our menu will appear. A value of `1000` is sufficiently large to ensure that no other HTML elements will come close to dethroning our menu as the topmost item on the page. #westeros

Conclusion

Now…you are finally done with learning how to create a sliding menu! This is one of my favorite examples because it not only explains how to create a common (and practical) UI component, but also contains a little bit of everything we've been talking about all of this time—CSS transitions, JavaScript modifying CSS, dealing with browser quirks around eventing, and more!

As you'll keep seeing in the future, ensuring that an animation plays when you change a property value is the easy part. Implementing everything around it that supports the property change is where things get tricky.

CHAPTER 11

Scroll-Activated Animations

For centuries, whenever you scrolled down a page full of content, nothing exciting happened. The content you scrolled into view just appeared. The content that you scrolled out of view just disappeared. The most exciting thing really was being able to use your fingers to scroll on touch devices as opposed to relying only on those gray scroll bars that annoyingly clung to the edges of your screen. Blech.

With improvements in CSS and the DOM APIs, something even more exciting became possible. Instead of talking about that, let me show you! If you have access to a browser, visit *http://bit.ly/ scroll_animation_example*.

Notice what happens once you start scrolling through the content. Depending on how far and how fast you are scrolling and what content is currently visible, you are going to see all sorts of awesomeness in the form of animations where your background color changes, content slides in from all directions, things fade into view, and so on. There is a name for all of these animations that play as you are scrolling, and that awfully boring name is *scroll-activated animations*.

In the following sections, you'll learn all about scroll-activated animations and the various techniques we can use to bring scrolled elements to life. The way we'll do that is by first taking a bird's-eye view of the problem and what our solution will look like. Then, we will look at some snippets of code in isolation before tying everything together and looking at how our scrolling example was created. This is gonna be a fun one, so let's get started.

The Basic Idea

The way scroll-activated animations work is pretty simple—up until the point where it gets kinda frustrating. The easy part just involves putting together a few technical pieces. The hard part involves figuring out how those technical pieces actually work, but we'll make sense of it all together in the following sections.

The Content

Starting at the top, the first thing to point out is your content:

Your content!

There isn't really anything special to call out here. Almost all of your pages, unless you specifically designed against it, will have more content than will fit on a single view. The way you bring the rest of the content into view is by scrolling. That brings us to our next step.

It's Scrolling Time

Your content by itself is pretty self-contained, but the way we view this content is by relying on our trusty browser (or WebView or equivalent doodad). Whenever your browser encounters more content than what it can display in one go, it will provide you with a means to scroll through the content:

Scrolling needed!!!

These *means* could be a touch gesture on a phone, a mouse/keyboard/scroll bar combination on a traditional computer, a game-pad on a video game console, or any host of input methods all the cool kids use these days. During this scrolling party, we want to modify our content by having the elements that scroll into view do different things.

Identifying the Elements

This is the hard part. We have been talking about the thing we scroll very generically as just *the content*. Our content is really made up of HTML elements—many *many* of them depending on how complex your page is. At any point, only a subset of all the HTML elements on the page will be visible inside your browser:

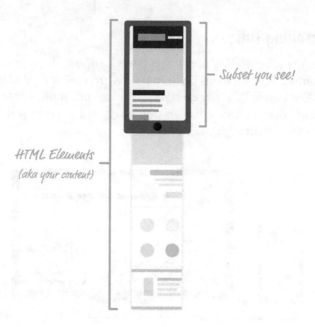

As you are scrolling, that subset of HTML elements that are visible will change:

Depending on what kind of an effect you are going for, figuring out which elements are visible is important. There are two (very closely related) approaches you can take for this. One approach involves simply checking whether *any part* of an element is visible:

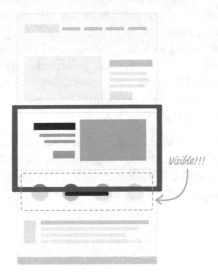

The other approach involves checking whether an element is *fully* visible:

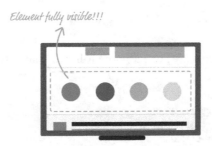

While the difference between both of these approaches seems subtle, the end result of whatever effect you decide to apply to your elements will be noticeably different.

Modifying the Elements

Now that you have identified the elements you want to affect, the last step is to actually do something with those elements. While the gist of this chapter is about animating the elements that scroll into view, the actual solution is more generic. This generic solution revolves around setting a class value on those now-visible elements. Doing this serves only one purpose: to activate any CSS style rules that now get applied because this class value got added to these elements. This is the basic concept behind styling elements using JavaScript that we saw earlier.

If you are not familiar with this concept (especially as it might pertain to scrolling), the previous paragraph is a lot to digest and wrap your head around. Let's walk through an example. First, we are going to start with some list elements:

```
<ol id="myList">
  <li>One</li>
  <li>Two</li>
  <li>Three</li>
  <li>Four</li>
  <li>Five</li>
  <li>Six</li>
  <li>Seven</li>
  <li>Eight</li>
  <li>Nine</li>
  <li>Ten</li>
</ol>
```

These list elements are styled by the following style rules:

```
#myList li {
  padding-left: 7px;
  margin-bottom: 15px;
  transition: all .2s ease-in-out;
  transform: translate3d(0px, 30px, 0);
  opacity: 0;
}
#myList li.active {
  transform: translate3d(0px, 0, 0);
  opacity: 1;
}
```

In our list items' current state, only the #myList li style rule is going to be applied on them. As you scroll some of these list items into view, we want these now-visible items to be styled a little bit differently to set them apart from the nonvisible list items. The way we do that is by giving these visible items a class value of `active`:

```
<ol id="myList">
<li class="active">One</li>
<li class="active">Two</li>
<li>Three</li>
<li>Four</li>
<li>Five</li>
<li>Six</li>
<li>Seven</li>
<li>Eight</li>
<li>Nine</li>
<li>Ten</li>
</ol>
```

The reason we do this isn't to have our elements look different in the HTML. At least, that isn't our end goal. The end goal is to have them be styled differently. The moment our visible list elements get a class value of `active` set, the `#myList li.activestyle` rule becomes active on them. This is the crucial difference that separates our visible elements from our nonvisible elements that don't have the `active` class set on them.

The rest is just gravy. More specifically, what we see depends entirely on what the various applied CSS rules specify, whether you have any transitions applied, and whether any properties your transitions are listening for get modified. For our example, when the `#myList li.active` style rule gets applied on the visible list items, those items will smoothly fade in and slide up. Why? You can thank the following highlighted lines in our CSS:

```
#myList li {
    padding-left: 7px;
    margin-bottom: 15px;
    transition: all .2s ease-in-out;
    transform: translate3d(0px, 30px, 0);
    opacity: 0;
}
#myList li.active {
    transform: translate3d(0px, 0, 0);
    opacity: 1;
}
```

If we had to visualize this, it might look something like the following:

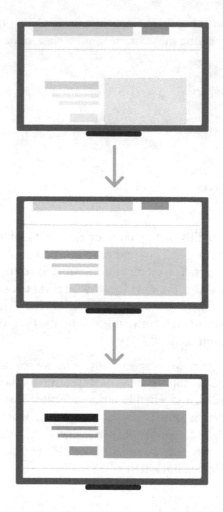

The important thing to note is that what happens is directly related to what CSS properties you specified in your style rules. Our fiddling with class values on visible elements is simply a signal. How your CSS reacts to that signal is entirely up to you, and you can very easily do far cooler and crazier things than the simple slide and fade-in that we've seen here! Creating these *scroll-activated animations* is just one part of the many things you can do!

Building It All Out

In the previous section, you learned about the various steps we will need to take to make our content come alive when scrolling. What we didn't get into were the specifics of how exactly we would implement in JavaScript all the cool things we saw. That's OK. We'll fix that up in this section.

Listening to the Scroll Event

The first piece of JavaScript we will look at revolves around detecting when you are scrolling. Whenever you scroll your page using the scroll bar (or fingers on a touch device), your browser fires the `scroll` event. The most straightforward way to listen and deal with this event is by doing something like the following:

```javascript
window.addEventListener("scroll", dealWithScrolling, false);

function dealWithScrolling(e) {
  // do epic stuff
}
```

Each time you scroll your browser window, the `dealWithScrolling` event handler will get called. Seems pretty simple, right?

There is one big problem with this approach. This event is very chatty. It gets called at a very high frequency, so you want to avoid manipulating the DOM or doing something very computationally intensive by reacting to the `scroll` event each time it gets called. While we can't slow down how quickly our browser fires the `scroll` event, we can control the frequency with which we react to it. You can use `setTimeOut` or `setInterval` to insert an artificial delay, but an even better solution is to peg our reactions to the frame rate. We can do that by relying on our old friend, `requestAnimationFrame`.

Take a look at the following snippet:

```javascript
var isScrolling = false;

window.addEventListener("scroll", throttleScroll, false);

function throttleScroll(e) {
  if (isScrolling == false ) {
    requestAnimationFrame(function() {
      dealWithScrolling(e);
      isScrolling = false;
    });
  }
  isScrolling = true;
}

function dealWithScrolling(e) {
```

```
    // do epic stuff
  }
```

The end result of this code running is identical to the direct approach you saw earlier. As your content gets scrolled, the deal WithScrolling event handler will get called. The difference is that your event handler won't get called faster than the frame rate as determined by the requestAnimationFrame method. This means that your event handler code will get called around 60 times a second—which is a good upper bound for the sorts of DOM-related things we will be doing anyway.

Detecting When Elements Are Visible

The only other snippets of code you need are for figuring out when elements are visible as you are scrolling. To do this, we will rely on two built-in helpers. The first one is getBoundingClientRect. This method returns the bounding box for whatever element we are interested in, and it provides position values for top, left, bottom, and right relative to your browser window's top-left corner in addition to the width and height properties. The second helper is the window.innerHeight and window.innerWidth properties, which return our browser height and width, respectively.

You can visualize all of this with the following diagram:

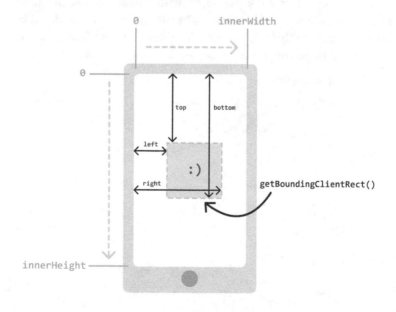

Take a few moments to make sense of what these properties and method do to help you figure out whether an element is in view or not. Once you've done this, let's look at the code needed to detect whether an element is partially or fully visible.

Detecting whether an element is partially visible

To detect whether any part of an element we are interested in is visible, you have the isPartiallyVisible function:

```
function isPartiallyVisible(el) {
    var elementBoundary = el.getBoundingClientRect();

    var top = elementBoundary.top;
    var bottom = elementBoundary.bottom;
    var height = elementBoundary.height;

    return ((top + height >= 0) &&
            (height + window.innerHeight >= bottom));
}
```

To use this function, pass in an element as an argument. If the element is partially visible, this function will return true. Otherwise, this function will return false.

Detecting whether an element is fully visible

To detect whether an element is fully visible, we have the isFullyVisible function:

```
function isFullyVisible(el) {
  var elementBoundary = el.getBoundingClientRect();

  var top = elementBoundary.top;
  var bottom = elementBoundary.bottom;

  return ((top >= 0) && (bottom <= window.innerHeight));
}
```

This function works very similarly to the isPartiallyVisible function. If the element we are checking is fully visible, our isFully Visible function will return true. If the element we are checking isn't visible or is only partially visible, this function will return false.

Putting It All Together

At this point, you have a good idea of how to make your content do cool and interesting things when you are scrolling through it. You also saw the handful of code snippets you will need to use to react to the scroll event and detect whether an element is visible or not by using the isPartiallyVisible and isFullyVisible functions. To see all of these things working together, it's easiest for us to view the source for the example from earlier. You can view it in its own separate page at *https://www.kirupa.com/animations/examples/animate_scroll.htm.*

If you want to just view the full HTML, CSS, and JS for our example, here you go:

```html
<!DOCTYPE html>
<html>

<head>
  <meta name="viewport"
        content="width=device-width, initial-scale=1.0" />
  <title>Change Color on Scroll</title>

  <style>
    body {
      background-color: #FDE74C;
      transition: all 1s ease-in;
      padding: 50px;
      color: #111;
      font-family: sans-serif;
      line-height: 32px;
      font-size: 18px;
    }

    h1 {
      font-family: sans-serif;
    }

    .colorOne {
      background-color: #9BC53D;
      color: #000;
    }

    .colorTwo {
      background-color: #FFF;
      color: #000;
    }

    #mainContent {
```

```
      width: 420px;
      margin: 0 auto;
    }

    #mainContent p {
      padding: 20px;
    }

    #mainContent #firstBox {
      font-weight: bold;
      transform: translate3d(-30px, 0, 0);
      transition: all .5s ease-out;
      opacity: 0;
    }

    #mainContent #firstBox.active {
      background-color: #333;
      color: #FFF;
      transform: translate3d(0, 0, 0);
      opacity: 1;
    }

    #mainContent #secondBox {
      transition: all .2s ease-in-out;
      transform: translate3d(0, 30px, 0);
      opacity: 0;
    }

    #mainContent #secondBox.active {
      background-color: #1581AF;
      color: #FFF;
      transform: translate3d(0, 0, 0);
      opacity: 1;
    }

    #mainContent ol li {
      padding-left: 7px;
      margin-bottom: 15px;
      transition: all .2s ease-in-out;
      transform: translate3d(20px, 0, 0);
      opacity: 0;
    }

    #mainContent ol li.active {
      transform: translate3d(0px, 0, 0);
      opacity: 1;
    }
  </style>
</head>

<body>
```

```
<div id="mainContent">
  <h1>Scroll Down</h1>
  <p>Lorem ipsum dolor sit amet, consectetur adipiscing elit.
     Curabitur quis massa a arcu efficitur suscipit vehicula
     et risus.</p>
  <ol id="myList">
    <li>Nam sagittis est non enim ultrices elementum. </li>
    <li>Sed id ligula sed mi tempor ornare.</li>
    <li>Aenean feugiat risus eget sagittis volutpat. Proin quis
        orci a metus lacinia auctor eget id nisi.</li>
    <li>Donec pulvinar nunc feugiat semper consequat.</li>
    <li>Etiam cursus justo eget libero gravida, nec faucibus
        mauris posuere.</li>
    <li>In nec sem id libero egestas cursus vel a urna.</li>
    <li>Fusce pulvinar arcu eu lobortis egestas. Maecenas
        eleifend felis ut urna consectetur, et pellentesque
        mi molestie.</li>
    <li>Aliquam ut felis venenatis, dapibus ante non, gravida
        nulla.</li>
    <li>Donec consectetur quam in urna commodo, sed aliquet
        metus vehicula.</li>
    <li>Mauris eget est sit amet felis eleifend sagittis non id
        nulla.</li>
  </ol>
  <p id="firstBox">Phasellus tortor nisl, dapibus at posuere
     sed, tempor in massa. Pellentesque eu sodales orci,
     finibus congue libero. Mauris molestie bibendum
     posuere.</p>
  <p>Nunc blandit varius sapien quis ultrices. Vestibulum et
     consequat augue. Pellentesque et maximus nisl, sit amet
     dictum ante.</p>
  <p id="secondBox">Nullam magna augue, consequat eu augue ut,
     volutpat fringilla est. Ut commodo ac magna vulputate
     dictum.</p>
</div>

<script>
  var isScrolling = false;

  window.addEventListener("scroll", throttleScroll, false);

  function throttleScroll(e) {
    if (isScrolling == false) {
      window.requestAnimationFrame(function() {
        scrolling(e);
        isScrolling = false;
      });
    }
    isScrolling = true;
  }
```

```javascript
document.addEventListener("DOMContentLoaded",
          scrolling,
          false);

var listItems = document.querySelectorAll(
              "#mainContent ol li");
var firstBox = document.querySelector("#firstBox");
var secondBox = document.querySelector("#secondBox");

function scrolling(e) {

  if (isPartiallyVisible(firstBox)) {
    firstBox.classList.add("active");

    document.body.classList.add("colorOne");
    document.body.classList.remove("colorTwo");
  } else {
    document.body.classList.remove("colorOne");
    document.body.classList.remove("colorTwo");
  }

  if (isFullyVisible(secondBox)) {
    secondBox.classList.add("active");

    document.body.classList.add("colorTwo");
    document.body.classList.remove("colorOne");
  }

  for (var i = 0; i < listItems.length; i++) {
    var listItem = listItems[i];

    if (isPartiallyVisible(listItem)) {
      listItem.classList.add("active");
    } else {
      listItem.classList.remove("active");
    }
  }
}

function isPartiallyVisible(el) {
  var elementBoundary = el.getBoundingClientRect();

  var top = elementBoundary.top;
  var bottom = elementBoundary.bottom;
  var height = elementBoundary.height;

  return ((top + height >= 0) &&
         (height + window.innerHeight >= bottom));
}

function isFullyVisible(el) {
```

```
        var elementBoundary = el.getBoundingClientRect();

        var top = elementBoundary.top;
        var bottom = elementBoundary.bottom;

        return ((top >= 0) && (bottom <= window.innerHeight));
    }
  </script>
</body>

</html>
```

While the amount of code here may seem intimidating, take a closer look to see that it is all actually fairly simple. The interesting things happen on our body element, our list items, and the two content boxes. See if you can spot in the JavaScript where all of these elements are affected by our adding and removing class values on them. Of course, don't miss the isFullyVisible and isPartiallyVisible functions doing their thing as well! This example should highlight everything we've talked about so far.

Some Performance Considerations

Having your content animate in and out while you are scrolling is only cool if it doesn't negatively affect performance. If you run a performance profile on our example in your favorite browser's performance tools, you'll see the frame rate stays pretty consistently around 60 fps. That's great news. Even on a mobile device, the performance is pretty nice.

This doesn't mean that our code is perfect. There are some optimizations we've done that are consciously trying to improve performance. Throttling the scroll event handler is one example of that. There are some optimizations we *didn't* do at the risk of over-optimizing something whose performance is already good. For example, calling getBoundingClientRect is slow and causes repaints. Checking window.innerHeight triggers a repaint as well. There are somewhat tricky workarounds for these issues, but rather than unnecessarily optimizing what is already 60 fps, the code leaves these two potential issues as is.

Lastly, listening to the scroll event (and most touch events) has its own set of issues. Most browsers optimize page scrolling heavily, but listening for a scroll- or touch-related event ends up negating those optimizations. The reason has to do with event handlers. We can ignore a page scroll by listening to a mouse scroll or touch event and calling preventDefault. This means if there are any event handlers associated with mouse scroll or touch, *your browser has to wait* to fully execute any JavaScript associated with that event handler. This is despite most event handlers of this sort never actually cancelling the scrolling. This verification can (and often does) drag down performance.

One partial workaround is to not listen to the mouse scroll event and instead use requestAnimationFrame and constantly poll the position of all of our elements that we want scrolled into or out of view. While that seems to solve the browser scroll optimization problem, it didn't result in any meaningful performance gains. Worse, calling getBoundingClientRect and window.innerHeight 60 times a second even if there are no scrolling or style-related changes created unnecessary work. Of course, this doesn't help with touch events at all. Sigh!

There is a bunch of good news, though! All of these issues are being fiddled with by a bunch of smart people at the W3C (World Wide Web Consortium) and the browser vendors, so we will have a much cleaner solution in the future. Keep an eye out for the following under-development features:

Passive event listeners
This feature adds an event property to specify, among other things, whether it will cancel a scroll or not. This means your browser can safely optimize scroll performance even if you are directly listening for the scroll event.

IntersectionObserver
The bulk of our code revolves around detecting whether an element is fully or partially visible as you scroll. This involves, as previously mentioned, expensive operations like getBounding ClientRect and window.innerHeight. The IntersectionOb server API solves this by bypassing these expensive operations. Instead, it provides specialized functionality for really efficiently detecting where an element is in relation to what you see on the screen.

Once those two technologies become more mainstream, this chapter will be revised in a future edition to fully take advantage of them. Until then, make sure to profile and measure the performance of your scroll-activated animation implementation to ensure everything runs properly. If it doesn't, drop a message on the forums (*http://forum.kirupa.com*) and we can look at what reasonable optimizations we can make.

Conclusion

Now that you have gone through this entire chapter, you've seen that doing interesting things when scrolling really only involves a few steps. You listen for the scroll event. You react to the scroll event by checking which elements are visible. On the visible elements, you toggle class values on them to allow different style rules to get applied. Separately, you need to ensure you have CSS style rules defined with selectors that become active when you toggle class values on the elements. Actually, now that we see everything involved, that is a lot of steps. Fortunately, only a handful of steps were new to you. The rest of the steps were just taking what you already knew and arranging it in a slightly different way. At least, that is what I like to tell myself.

CHAPTER 12

The iOS Icon Wobble/Jiggle

When you press and hold an icon on your iOS (iPhone/iPad/iPod) device's home screen, you'll get the ability to rearrange the icons or uninstall the app associated with it. That's really boring and not the interesting part I want you to focus on. The interesting part is what these icons do as a result of you pressing and holding. They wobble and jiggle (aka wobiggle) around. It's pretty awesome.

Anyway, I thought it would be fun to re-create that effect. After about 30 minutes of fiddling around, you can see my attempt as a very unhelpful static screenshot in Figure 12-1 (or in your browser at *http://bit.ly/iOSWobble*):

Figure 12-1. A static representation of what we will be creating; imagine each of these icons is wobbling around

In my very humble opinion, this implementation is really *really* close to what you see on an iOS device.

Anyway, in this deconstruction, you will learn all about how this effect works. It's going to be a lotta fun. Before you proceed, just make sure you are up-to-date on working with *nth-child selectors* (*http://bit.ly/nthChild*). Otherwise, your fun will be lessened by a great deal of confusion and possibly crying. You have been warned.

The Full HTML and CSS

Before we go any further, let me throw at you all of the HTML and CSS that makes this example work:

```html
<!DOCTYPE html>
<html>

<head>
  <title>iPhone / iPad Icon Wobble Effect</title>
  <style>
    body {
      background-color: #EFEFEF;
      padding: 25px;
    }

    #main {
      width: 450px;
    }

    #main .icon {
      padding: 20px;
      border-radius: 40px;
    }

    #main .icon:nth-child(2n) {
      animation-name: keyframes1;
      animation-iteration-count: infinite;
      transform-origin: 50% 10%;
    }

    #main .icon:nth-child(2n-1) {
      animation-name: keyframes2;
      animation-iteration-count: infinite;
      animation-direction: alternate;
      transform-origin: 30% 5%;
    }

    @keyframes keyframes1 {
      0% {
```

```
        transform: rotate(-1deg);
        animation-timing-function: ease-in;
      }
      50% {
        transform: rotate(1.5deg);
        animation-timing-function: ease-out;
      }
    }

    @keyframes keyframes2 {
      0% {
        transform: rotate(1deg);
        animation-timing-function: ease-in;
      }
      50% {
        transform: rotate(-1.5deg);
        animation-timing-function: ease-out;
      }
    }
  </style>
</head>

<body>
  <div id="main">
    <img class="icon"
         style="animation-delay: -.75s; animation-duration: .25s"
         height="100"
         src="http://www.kirupa.com/images/icon1.png"
         width="100">
    <img class="icon"
         style="animation-delay: -.5s; animation-duration: .3s"
         height="100"
         src="http://www.kirupa.com/images/icon2.png"
         width="100">
    <img class="icon"
         style=" animation-delay: -.05s; animation-duration: .27s"
         height="100"
         src="http://www.kirupa.com/images/icon3.png"
         width="100">
    <img class="icon"
         style="animation-delay: -.2s; animation-duration: .33s"
         height="100"
         src="http://www.kirupa.com/images/icon4.png"
         width="100">
    <img class="icon"
         style="animation-delay: -.31s; animation-duration: .24s"
         height="100"
         src="http://www.kirupa.com/images/icon7.png"
         width="100">
    <img class="icon"
         style="animation-delay: -.15s; animation-duration: .25s"
```

```
            height="100"
            src="http://www.kirupa.com/images/icon5.png"
            width="100">
    <img class="icon"
            style="animation-delay: -.2s; animation-duration: .22s"
            height="100"
            src="http://www.kirupa.com/images/icon6.png"
            width="100">
    <img class="icon"
            style="animation-delay: -.3s; animation-duration: .28s"
            height="100"
            src="http://www.kirupa.com/images/icon8.png"
            width="100">
    <img class="icon"
            style="animation-delay: -.22s; animation-duration: .3s"
            height="100"
            src="http://www.kirupa.com/images/icon9.png"
            width="100">
    </div>
    </body>

    </html>
```

Take a few moments to skim through all of this. Don't worry if everything doesn't make sense yet. That's what the remaining sections are there to help you out with.

Deconstructing This Effect

Before we get to the implementation details, let's take a few steps back and look at what exactly this animation is doing. As you will see soon enough, this animation really isn't doing much, because the wobble is really nothing more than a rotation. Srsly!

The reason you may find this surprising is that we commonly think of a rotation as what's shown in Figure 12-2.

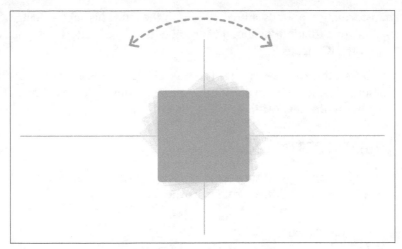

Figure 12-2. What a traditional rotation looks like

The item you are rotating pivots around its vertical and horizontal center point—the key word being *center*. See, the thing is, that doesn't always have to be the case. By moving the point your item rotates around to somewhere other than the center of the object, you can end up with something that looks like Figure 12-3.

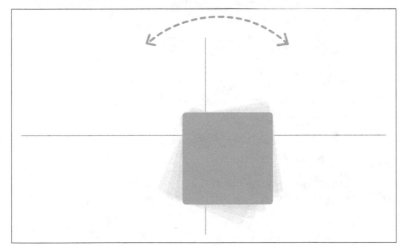

Figure 12-3. By shifting the point we rotate from, you can create something slightly more unique!

Notice that our object is still rotating. It's just that what it is rotating around isn't the center point anymore. To describe it more formally, the *transformation point* is no longer the center of the object. The transformation point is shifted up and to the left. This subtle change makes your rotation look a bit more like the wobble effect that you see on the iOS icons.

Of course, this isn't everything. There is a little bit more to your animation, like the duration and easing function, but we'll look at them shortly...in the next section!

Looking at the CSS

This effect and everything we've covered so far is implemented entirely using CSS animations. Here's the relevant CSS:

```css
#main {
  width: 450px;
}

#main .icon {
  padding: 20px;
  border-radius: 40px;
}

#main .icon:nth-child(2n) {
  animation-name: keyframes1;
  animation-iteration-count: infinite;
  transform-origin: 50% 10%;
}

#main .icon:nth-child(2n-1) {
  animation-name: keyframes2;
  animation-iteration-count: infinite;
  animation-direction: alternate;
  transform-origin: 30% 5%;
}

@keyframes keyframes1 {
  0% {
    transform: rotate(-1deg);
    animation-timing-function: ease-in;
  }
  50% {
    transform: rotate(1.5deg);
    animation-timing-function: ease-out;
  }
}

@keyframes keyframes2 {
  0% {
    transform: rotate(1deg);
```

```
    animation-timing-function: ease-in;
  }
  50% {
    transform: rotate(-1.5deg);
    animation-timing-function: ease-out;
  }
}
```

Take a few more moments to read through the CSS. Nothing should be too surprising, but let's look at the interesting parts.

The rotation is handled in the keyframes via the `transform` property's `rotate` function:

```
@keyframes keyframes2 {
  0% {
    transform: rotate(1deg);
    animation-timing-function: ease-in;
  }
  50% {
    transform: rotate(-1.5deg);
    animation-timing-function: ease-out;
  }
}
```

The easing function (aka `animation-timing-function`) is an `ease-in` as you are going through the rotation, and it is an `ease-out` as you return to the starting point. Keyframes by themselves aren't very useful, as they need to have the animation property declared somewhere and referring to them. That referring (among other important things) is handled by the two nearly identical `#main` `.icon` style rules—one of which you see here:

```
#main .icon:nth-child(2n-1) {
  animation-name: keyframes2;
  animation-iteration-count: infinite;
  animation-direction: alternate;
  transform-origin: 30% 5%;
}
```

The only line to call out here is the `transform-origin` property. This is the very important property (VIP) that allows you to specify the center point where a transformation such as your rotate will actually take place. It is this property that offsets your icon's transformation point and turns your simple rotation into a slight wobble.

So far, so good, right?

Faking Randomness

Now, the challenge with implementing this effect entirely in CSS is that you can't really have randomness in how things move. Everything has to be predetermined. Despite this constraint, there are a few things you can do to help make each image wobble with a little uniqueness so that you don't get something that looks really mechanical and fake.

Slightly Different Variants of Style Rules + Keyframes

The first (and most obvious) of the "few things" is that, if you look at your CSS, you'll notice that it doesn't have just a single animation declaration and corresponding keyframes. Instead, it has two of each.

The style rules containing the animation declarations look as follows:

```
#main .icon:nth-child(2n) {
  animation-name: keyframes1;
  animation-iteration-count: infinite;
  transform-origin: 50% 10%;
}

#main .icon:nth-child(2n-1) {
  animation-name: keyframes2;
  animation-iteration-count: infinite;
  animation-direction: alternate;
  transform-origin: 30% 5%;
}
```

The keyframes associated with these animation declarations are:

```
@keyframes keyframes1 {
  0% {
    transform: rotate(-1deg);
    animation-timing-function: ease-in;
  }
  50% {
    transform: rotate(1.5deg);
    animation-timing-function: ease-out;
  }
}

@keyframes keyframes2 {
  0% {
    transform: rotate(1deg);
    animation-timing-function: ease-in;
```

```
    }
  50% {
    transform: rotate(-1.5deg);
    animation-timing-function: ease-out;
  }
}
```

Notice that there are subtle differences in each of the variants. In one animation, you rotate from –1 degrees to 1.5 degrees. In the other, you rotate from 1 degree to –1.5 degrees. The `transform-origin` property that determines the center point of your rotation is also different, and one of the animations is set to alternate its direction.

Which element gets which animation version is handled by the *n*th-child pseudoselector, which is happily attached to the `#main` `.icon` style rules. The *n*th-child selector with `2n` will select every even-numbered element. The nth-child selector with `2n-1` will select every odd-numbered element. The end result is that every icon will alternatively get one variant of the animation declaration.

Unfortunately, having each icon animate in one of two ways isn't different enough. You'll quickly find yourself staring at a wall of icons that move in sync. That isn't going to look nice, and we certainly don't want to bloat our CSS with a lot of slightly different copies of what we already have right now. Even the two copies we have right now are a bit overkill!

Altering Some CSS Properties and Their Values...Inline!

The way to account for this monotonous movement is our second of the "few things." Here, we specify some key animation properties inline on the icons themselves:

```
<div id="main">
  <img class="icon"
       style="animation-delay: -.75s; animation-duration: .25s"
       height="100"
       src="http://www.kirupa.com/images/icon1.png"
       width="100">
  <img class="icon"
       style="animation-delay: -.5s; animation-duration: .3s"
       height="100"
       src="http://www.kirupa.com/images/icon2.png"
       width="100">
  <img class="icon"
       style="animation-delay: -.05s; animation-duration: .27s"
```

```
            height="100"
            src="http://www.kirupa.com/images/icon3.png"
            width="100">
            .
            .
            .

    <img class="icon"
        style="animation-delay: -.22s; animation-duration: .3s"
        height="100"
        src="http://www.kirupa.com/images/icon9.png"
        width="100">
</div>
```

Notice that each `img` element has the `animation-delay` and `animation-duration` properties set to slightly different values.

A negative value for the `animation-delay` property determines how many seconds into the animation to actually start playing. It's basically an offset. The `animation-duration` property is easier to comprehend. It specifies how long the animation will actually play.

By altering the values on these two properties for each element, we can ensure a certain level of non-uniformity in how the animation plays across all of the icons. This, combined with our alternating animation variants, gives us a pretty compelling simulation of random behavior using only CSS.

Conclusion

This effect can be summed up as follows: it is an off-center rotation. That's it. The iOS wobble effect, as you can see, is pretty straightforward (and little less exciting) once you simplify the animation down to its technical parts. In fact, the bulk of the markup isn't actually there to re-create the effect. Most of what you see is devoted entirely to helping all of our icons move in a slightly unique way…aka trying to fake randomness using CSS.

For true randomness, you need to employ some JavaScript. You can make a pretty compelling case that the approach I explained is a bit inefficient. You could argue that it would be better to specify some of the animation parameters in code instead of largely duplicating style rules or specifying inline styles. For example, instead of specifying inline styles for the `animation-delay` and `animation-duration` properties on each image, we could have specified them

entirely in code using a single `for` loop and our friendly `Math.ran`
`dom` function.

Ultimately, there is no right or wrong way to tackle this. For the
handful of images you see here, just doing everything in CSS seemed
fine. Now, if you are going to be applying this effect to a lot of elements, specifying inline styles for each element can get pretty tedi-
ous. In that scenario, I highly encourage you to go the JavaScript
route.

CHAPTER 13

Parallax Scrolling

For many practical reasons, our UIs are designed to be two dimensional and flat. Once you throw in meaningful content, some navigation, and other doodads to make your application usable, adding any more dimensions simply gets in the way and becomes a distraction. Despite the stranglehold two dimensions have on what we create, there are subtle and effective ways of sneaking an extra dimension in here and there.

In this deconstruction, I will show you one effective way where you can simulate depth by implementing something known as the *parallax effect*. Before I bore you by explaining what parallax is, let's look at an example instead. Load up your browser, and visit *http://bit.ly/ parallax_scrolling*.

When the example loads, you'll see something that looks like this:

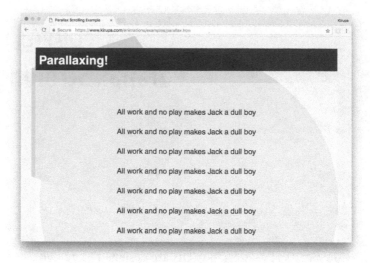

You'll see some content that will require you to scroll to fully reach the end of the page. In the background, you will find various shapes. When you scroll the page, cool things happen!

Notice what is happening to the background while you are scrolling. There's a big yellow circle that moves much slower than your scroll speed, a blue square that scrolls much faster than your scroll speed, and a green hexagon shape (which you can barely see) that moves in the direction of your scrolling. All of these variations in speed create the illusion of depth, making it look like the various background elements are located at various distances, and giving our content some extra depth. Bam! That's some sweet parallax at work here.

In the following sections, you will not only re-create this parallax effect, but you'll also learn all about how it works so that you can take advantage of it in your own projects.

What Exactly Is Parallax?

Generically speaking, *parallax* is the name for the illusion where objects' positions seem to be shifted based on the angle at which you are viewing them. Have you ever noticed when you are driving that things farther away seem to move slower than things closer to you? That's an example of parallax where your orientation to your surroundings affects your perception of how far things move.

To learn more about parallax, head on over to the ultimate author-ity on all things parallax, Wikipedia (*http://en.wikipedia.org/wiki/Parallax*)!

Overview of How the Parallax Effect Works

Before we start looking at the sweet implementation that makes our example rock, let's take a few steps back and talk about how exactly this effect works. As you will see in a few moments, it's pretty simple. It just takes advantage of a few techniques that you normally don't see being used together in this context.

For our parallax effect, we need a way to independently move our background elements and content when the entire page is scrolled. We do this by *layering*. We layer our background elements directly behind our content like so:

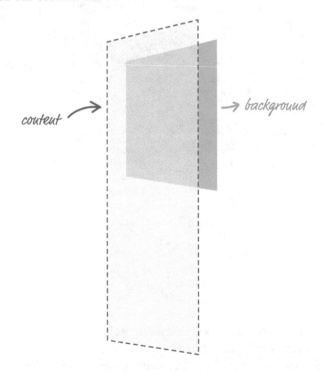

There are several reasons why we do this—some obvious, and some not so obvious:

- First, your content will not interfere in any way with what is happening behind the scenes.
- Second, you can squeeze in a lot of performance by doing this—something we will discuss toward the end of this deconstruction.
- Lastly (and most importantly), with this arrangement, when you scroll the browser window, the content position and background elements' positions can be adjusted independently very easily:

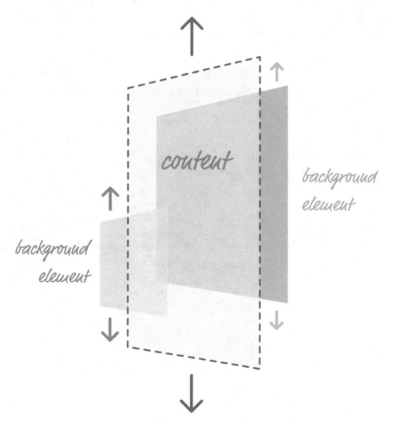

The next thing to look at is the scrolling itself. There are at least four ways you can scroll content in a browser: by using the scroll bars, by using the mouse wheel, by using your fingers (on mobile devices), and by using the up/down/PgUp/PgDn/etc. keys on your keyboard.

Regardless of how you scroll your page, when you do, everything on your page moves up or down by default. The amount it moves may vary depending on whether you used the scroll bar, fingers, mouse wheel, or keyboard, but rest assured that everything on your page will move. The thing is, we don't want our background elements to automatically move when we scroll our browser. We want to control how much our background elements scroll (and in which direction) ourselves.

The solution is simple. We simply prevent our background elements from scrolling with the rest of the page:

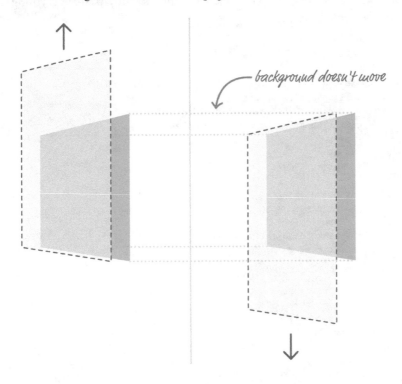

background doesn't move

With this change, we can adjust our background element positions as we see fit.

The last step that remains is actually shifting our background elements' positions. We do this by paying attention to how much we have scrolled our browser window. Depending on how far we have scrolled (or are currently scrolling), we adjust our background elements' positions accordingly. That sounds pretty simple, and as it turns out…it actually is!

In the following sections, we'll take all of these words and turn them into working HTML, CSS, and JavaScript to bring our parallax effect to life.

Getting Started

Now that you have an understanding of how this effect works, the next step is to get this example working on your own computer. Go ahead and create a new HTML document and copy/paste everything you see here into it:

```html
<!DOCTYPE html>
<html>

<head>
  <meta name="viewport"
      content="width=device-width, initial-scale=1.0"/>
  <title>Parallax Scrolling Example</title>
  <style>
    body {
      background-color: #EEE;
    }
    #content {
      padding: 50px;
      margin: 40px;
      background-color: rgba(255, 255, 255, .48);
      text-align: center;
    }
    #content p {
      font-family: Helvetica, sans-serif;
      font-size: 28px;
      line-height: 40px;
      color: #111;
    }
    h1 {
      text-transform: capitalize;
      font-family: sans-serif;
      font-size: 40px;
      padding: 10px;
      margin: 40px;
      background-color: rgba(20, 20, 20, .8);
      color: #FFF;
    }
  </style>
</head>

<body>
  <h1>Parallaxing!</h1>
  <div id="content">
```

```
    <p>All work and no play makes Jack a dull boy</p>
    <p>All work and no play makes Jack a dull boy</p>
    <p>All work and no play makes Jack a dull boy</p>
    <p>All work and no play makes Jack a dull boy</p>
    <p>All work and no play makes Jack a dull boy</p>
    <p>All work and no play makes Jack a dull boy</p>
    <p>All work and no play makes Jack a dull boy</p>
    <p>All work and no play makes Jack a dull boy</p>
    <p>All work and no play makes Jack a dull boy</p>
    <p>All work and no play makes Jack a dull boy</p>
    <p>All work and no play makes Jack a dull boy</p>
    <p>All work and no play makes Jack a dull boy</p>
    <p>All work and no play makes Jack a dull boy</p>
    <p>All work and no play makes Jack a dull boy</p>
    <p>All work and no play makes Jack a dull boy</p>
    <p>All work and no play makes Jack a dull boy</p>
    <p>All work and no play makes Jack a dull boy</p>
    <p>All work and no play makes Jack a dull boy</p>
    <p>All work and no play makes Jack a dull boy</p>
    <p>All work and no play makes Jack a dull boy</p>
    <p>All work and no play makes Jack a dull boy</p>
  </div>

  <script>

  </script>
  </body>

  </html>
```

Once you've added all of this HTML, CSS, and JavaScript, save your
document and preview what you have in your browser. You'll see an
example that looks almost like what we saw earlier without the background elements and the parallax effect. Those are things that we'll
be adding together.

Adding Our Background Elements

The first thing we are going to do is add our background elements.
Our background elements are nothing more than div elements that
are absolutely positioned. In our HTML just above the opening
script tag, add the following lines:

```
<div id="bigYellowCircle"></div>
<div id="blueSquare"></div>
<div id="greenPentagon"></div>
```

What we are doing is adding three div elements, each with an id
value of bigYellowCircle, blueSquare, and greenPentagon. There

really isn't much going on here; the real work takes place in the CSS. Inside our style region, add the following style rules:

```css
#bigYellowCircle {
  background-image: url("http://bit.ly/yellowCircle");
  background-repeat: no-repeat;
  background-position: center center;
  background-size: 90%;
  position: fixed;
  top: 0;
  width: 100vw;
  height: 100vh;
  z-index: -1;
  opacity: .75;
}
#blueSquare {
  background-image: url("http://bit.ly/blueSquare");
  background-repeat: no-repeat;
  background-position: 97% bottom;
  background-size: 10%;
  position: fixed;
  top: 0;
  width: 100vw;
  height: 100vh;
  z-index: -2;
  opacity: .75;
}
#greenPentagon {
  background-image: url("http://bit.ly/greenPentagon");
  background-repeat: no-repeat;
  background-position: 5% top;
  background-size: 50%;
  position: fixed;
  top: 0;
  width: 100vw;
  height: 100vh;
  z-index: -3;
  opacity: .75;
}
```

These style rules affect the three div elements we just added. Take a look at the properties we are setting on them. The shapes you see are background images. Each div element takes up the full size of the viewport, and we adjust the position and size of each background image to get the final effect.

If you save your document now and preview it in your browser, you'll notice that these background images appear. When you scroll the page, the content scrolls. The background elements stay fixed.

The background elements also appear behind our content. Let's go back to our CSS!

To ensure our background elements stay fixed, we set the `position` CSS property to `fixed`. To ensure our background elements appear behind our content, we set the `z-index` property to a negative value like `-1`, `-2`, or `-3` for each of our `div` elements.

For example, here are these two properties highlighted for our `#greenPentagon` style rule:

```
#greenPentagon {
  background-image: url("http://bit.ly/greenPentagon");
  background-repeat: no-repeat;
  background-position: 5% top;
  background-size: 50%;
  position: fixed;
  top: 0;
  width: 100vw;
  height: 100vh;
  z-index: -3;
  opacity: .75;
}
```

At this point, we've taken care of ensuring our background elements are represented in HTML and CSS properly. All that remains is adding the JavaScript to adjust their positions as we are scrolling.

The JavaScript

Inside our `script` tags, we will add the code that will:

1. Listen for our current scroll position.
2. Slide our background elements up or down using a `translate3d` transform with vertical values based on the current scroll position.

We will write this code gradually and talk about what is happening at each step.

Referencing our background elements

The first thing we are going to do is reference our background elements in code so that we can access them easily. Inside our `script` tags, add the following three lines:

```
var bigYellowCircle = document.querySelector("#bigYellowCircle");
var blueSquare = document.querySelector("#blueSquare");
var greenPentagon = document.querySelector("#greenPentagon");
```

This should be pretty straightforward. We are storing our bigYellow
Circle, blueSquare, and greenPentagon elements in variables of
their same name using some help from the querySelector method.

Setting the Position

For reasons you've heard a bunch about already, we will be shifting
our background elements using a translate3d transform. In
CSS, the way we set translate3d looks as follows:

```
#blah {
    transform: translate3d(10px, 20px, 0);
}
```

What we need to do is create a JavaScript version that allows us to
do the same thing. To do that, below our existing code, add the
following:

```
function setTranslate(xPos, yPos, el) {
    el.style.transform = "translate3d(" + xPos + "px, "
                          + yPos + "px, 0)";
}
```

We just added a function called setTranslate, and it takes three
arguments: the horizontal position, vertical position, and the element to set the transform on. The second line lets us re-create the
translate3d transform while allowing the numerical values to be
specified by our arguments. It works. I swear!

ES6 Template Literals to the Rescue

If you don't like having to compose strings using all of those quotation marks, you may like ES6 template literals a whole lot. The previous setTranslate function using template literals will look as
follows:

```
function setTranslate(xPos, yPos, el) {
    el.style.transform = `translate3d(${xPos}px,
                                       ${yPos}px,
                                       0)`;
}
```

Looks much cleaner, right? Browser support is limited to only the newest releases, so you may want to wait a bit before using it or use a transpiler like Babel to support older browsers as well.

Getting the scroll position

The most complex part of our code deals with getting our scroll position and using that to update the position of our background elements. The first thing we'll do is add the code for getting the scroll position. Go ahead and add the following:

```
window.addEventListener("DOMContentLoaded", scrollLoop, false);

var xScrollPosition;
var yScrollPosition;

function scrollLoop() {
  xScrollPosition = window.scrollX;
  yScrollPosition = window.scrollY;

  requestAnimationFrame(scrollLoop);
}
```

There are a few things that happen with this code. The first thing we do is call a function named scrollLoop when our page's DOM has loaded:

```
window.addEventListener("DOMContentLoaded", scrollLoop, false);
```

This is all done by relying on the DOMContentLoaded event. The scrollLoop function is where all the magic happens, so let's look at that one next:

```
var xScrollPosition;
var yScrollPosition;

function scrollLoop() {
  xScrollPosition = window.scrollX;
  yScrollPosition = window.scrollY;

  requestAnimationFrame(scrollLoop);
}
```

We store the current scroll position in our xScrollPosition and yScrollPosition variables. We get the scroll position by accessing the window.scrollX and window.scrollY properties. So far, so good, right? Because these properties will change as we scroll our page, we need a way to keep our xScrollPosition and yScrollPosi tion variables up-to-date. That is where the requestAnimation Frame call comes in. It ensures we call our scrollLoop function every time our screen is ready to update—no slower, no faster.

The only thing that is missing is the part where we use all of this data to adjust the position of our background elements! To take care of that, add the following highlighted lines:

```
function scrollLoop() {
  xScrollPosition = window.scrollX;
  yScrollPosition = window.scrollY;

  setTranslate(0, yScrollPosition * -0.2, bigYellowCircle);
  setTranslate(0, yScrollPosition * -1.5, blueSquare);
  setTranslate(0, yScrollPosition * .5, greenPentagon);

  requestAnimationFrame(scrollLoop);
}
```

In these lines, we are calling the setTranslate function and passing in the values for the horizontal position, vertical position, and element to apply our translate3d transform to. Because we aren't shifting our background elements horizontally, the first argument is just 0. The second argument is where we pass our current vertical scroll position (aka yScrollPosition), and we multiply our position by a scale factor to adjust how fast, how slow, or in what direction our background elements will actually move. With these scale factors, you have a lot of room for experimentation, so feel free to go crazy if you want to. And with that, preview your page in the browser. Everything should work as expected. If it doesn't, here is the full markup and code for everything we've done:

```
<!DOCTYPE html>
<html>

<head>
  <meta name="viewport"
        content="width=device-width, initial-scale=1.0"/>
  <title>Parallax Scrolling Example</title>
  <style>
    body {
      background-color: #EEE;
    }
    #content {
      padding: 50px;
      margin: 40px;
      background-color: rgba(255, 255, 255, .48);
      text-align: center;
```

```
}
#content p {
  font-family: Helvetica, sans-serif;
  font-size: 28px;
  line-height: 40px;
  color: #111;
}
h1 {
  text-transform: capitalize;
  font-family: sans-serif;
  font-size: 40px;
  padding: 10px;
  margin: 40px;
  background-color: rgba(20, 20, 20, .8);
  color: #FFF;
}
#bigYellowCircle {
  background-image: url("http://bit.ly/yellowCircle");
  background-repeat: no-repeat;
  background-position: center center;
  background-size: 90%;
  position: fixed;
  top: 0;
  width: 100vw;
  height: 100vh;
  z-index: -1;
  opacity: .75;
}
#blueSquare {
  background-image: url("http://bit.ly/blueSquare");
  background-repeat: no-repeat;
  background-position: 97% bottom;
  background-size: 10%;
  position: fixed;
  top: 0;
  width: 100vw;
  height: 100vh;
  z-index: -2;
  opacity: .75;
}
#greenPentagon {
  background-image: url("http://bit.ly/greenPentagon");
  background-repeat: no-repeat;
  background-position: 5% top;
  background-size: 50%;
  position: fixed;
  top: 0;
  width: 100vw;
  height: 100vh;
  z-index: -3;
  opacity: .75;
```

```
      }
    </style>
</head>

<body>
  <h1>Parallaxing!</h1>
  <div id="content">
    <p>All work and no play makes Jack a dull boy</p>
    <p>All work and no play makes Jack a dull boy</p>
    <p>All work and no play makes Jack a dull boy</p>
    <p>All work and no play makes Jack a dull boy</p>
    <p>All work and no play makes Jack a dull boy</p>
    <p>All work and no play makes Jack a dull boy</p>
    <p>All work and no play makes Jack a dull boy</p>
    <p>All work and no play makes Jack a dull boy</p>
    <p>All work and no play makes Jack a dull boy</p>
    <p>All work and no play makes Jack a dull boy</p>
    <p>All work and no play makes Jack a dull boy</p>
    <p>All work and no play makes Jack a dull boy</p>
    <p>All work and no play makes Jack a dull boy</p>
    <p>All work and no play makes Jack a dull boy</p>
    <p>All work and no play makes Jack a dull boy</p>
    <p>All work and no play makes Jack a dull boy</p>
    <p>All work and no play makes Jack a dull boy</p>
    <p>All work and no play makes Jack a dull boy</p>
    <p>All work and no play makes Jack a dull boy</p>
    <p>All work and no play makes Jack a dull boy</p>
    <p>All work and no play makes Jack a dull boy</p>
  </div>

  <div id="bigYellowCircle"></div>
  <div id="blueSquare"></div>
  <div id="greenPentagon"></div>

  <script>
    var bigYellowCircle =
        document.querySelector("#bigYellowCircle");
    var blueSquare = document.querySelector("#blueSquare");
    var greenPentagon = document.querySelector("#greenPentagon");

    function setTranslate(xPos, yPos, el) {
      el.style.transform = "translate3d(" + xPos + "px, "
                           + yPos + "px, 0)";
    }

    window.addEventListener("DOMContentLoaded", scrollLoop, false);

    var xScrollPosition;
    var yScrollPosition;

    function scrollLoop() {
```

```
        xScrollPosition = window.scrollX;
        yScrollPosition = window.scrollY;

        setTranslate(0, yScrollPosition * -0.2, bigYellowCircle);
        setTranslate(0, yScrollPosition * -1.5, blueSquare);
        setTranslate(0, yScrollPosition * .5, greenPentagon);

        requestAnimationFrame(scrollLoop);
    }
  </script>
</body>

</html>
```

Double-check to make sure nothing is off—it's easy to make a typo, miss a comma, or have an uneven quotation mark!

What About xScrollPosition?

In our code, we declare and initialize a variable called `xScrollPosition`. Nowhere do we actually use this variable. The reason I included it is to make our `scrollLoop` function more generic and help you apply its magic to both horizontal and vertical scrolls.

Conclusion

There are a bunch of different ways to implement parallax scrolling. The one described here is more on the simpler side. As you can see, everything is done in fewer than 20 lines of code while still giving you a fair amount of flexibility in customizing how your background elements will scroll. The only thing to keep in mind is performance. The approach described here will scale to having hundreds of background elements sliding up, down, left, or right without killing your frame rate too much. As always, though, profile and measure to make sure!

CHAPTER 14

Sprite Sheet Animations Using Only CSS

Sprite sheets can be used for more than just optimizing how you display static images. Hearkening back to the very first arcade games, your sprite sheets can also be used to contain a sequence of images that make up the individual frames of an animation. When these frames are played back rapidly, what you see is a moving picture.

This is yet another example that is hard to show in book form, but you can see a live example at *http://bit.ly/sprite_animation*.

This animation relies on a single sprite sheet (*https://www.kirupa.com/html5/examples/images/sprites_final.png*) that contains the individual frames (aka a *sprite*) of the circles moving. Just a small portion of this sprite sheet looks a bit like Figure 14-1.

While creating all of this seems complicated, it really isn't. By the time you reach the end of this chapter, you will have learned how to combine a sprite sheet, a CSS animation, and the steps easing function to create the example just shown.

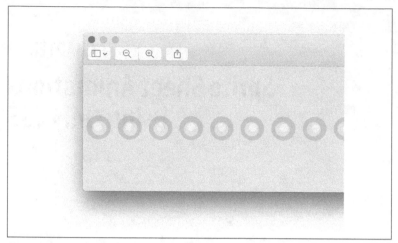

Figure 14-1. The sequence of images that make up your sprite sheet

Creating the Sprite Sheet

This one should be kinda obvious. Before you can animate sprites from a sprite sheet, *you first need a sprite sheet*. There are a variety of tools out there that help you with this, and my favorite is Flash Professional/Adobe Animate's Generate Sprite Sheet functionality:

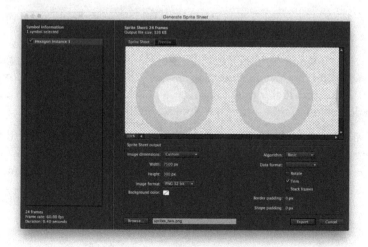

If you google around, you'll find many other solutions that people rave about. Covering how to create a sprite sheet goes beyond the scope of this book, but whatever tool you use, just make sure of two things:

- Each frame in your sprite sheet is evenly sized.
- The frames you wish to animate are arranged on a single row. Some tools like to break up the sprites into a single column or a combination of rows and columns! We don't want that.

Now, if you don't have a sprite sheet already created, don't worry. Just use the sprite sheet of the blue circles that I am using, from *https://www.kirupa.com/images/sprites_final.png.*

The Actual Implementation

Now we get to the good stuff. With your sprite sheet in tow, all that remains is to specify the HTML element the individual sprites will be shown through, get that element sized correctly, and finally specify the CSS animation. Let's tackle each part in the next few sections.

The HTML element

The first thing we need to do is create a div element that will act as the viewport for our animation. Create an HTML document, and add the following markup:

```
<!DOCTYPE html>
<html>

<head>
  <title>CSS Sprite Animation</title>
</head>

<body>
  <div id="spriteContainer"></div>
</body>

</html>
```

There is nothing interesting going on except for a div element whose id is spriteContainer. This is the element we will see our animation through, and that means we need to size this div element appropriately to ensure the frames of our sprite sheet display properly.

Properly sizing the HTML element

The width and height of this div need to match the size of a single frame in your sprite sheet. This will vary depending on how large your sprites are, but for our blue circles one, the width and height is going to be 300 pixels. Armed with this information, let's resize spriteContainer to the same size.

Add the following lines of CSS:

```
<!DOCTYPE html>
<html>

<head>
  <title>CSS Sprite Animation</title>
  <style>
    #spriteContainer {
      width: 300px;
      height: 300px;
      display: block;
    }
  </style>
</head>

<body>
  <div id="spriteContainer"></div>
</body>

</html>
```

The highlighted lines ensure that our spriteContainer div element is now sized just right. The next step is to get the first frame of our sprite sheet to appear.

Setting the background image

We get the first frame of the sprite to appear by setting the sprite Container element's background-image CSS property to the location of our sprite sheet. Modify the #spriteContainer style rule by adding the following line:

```
#spriteContainer {
  width: 300px;
  height: 300px;
  display: block;
  background-image: url("http://bit.ly/spriteImage");
}
```

Shortened Image URL

To make it easier to read, the link to the sprite image has been shortened in the preceding CSS snippet. If for whatever reason you need the full URL, it is *https://www.kirupa.com/html5/examples/images/sprites_final.png*.

My sprite sheet is called *sprites_final.png* and it is located inside the *images* folder. You should update the path to point to your image. Once you've made this change, preview your page in the browser:

If everything works properly, you should see the first frame of your sprite sheet displayed. If you aren't seeing that, something is wrong somewhere. The most likely cause is that you misspelled the path to the sprite sheet. It could also be gremlins. Never doubt a gremlin's ability to make your web development life difficult.

It's Animation Time

Right now, you have something that looks like this:

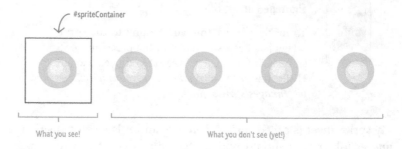

What you see!   What you don't see (yet!)

The first frame of the sprite is displayed as a background image, and the remaining frames are just out of view—itching to get a shot at the spotlight. The solution is simple. We need to slide the image left so that the rest of the frames get displayed. The way we are going to do that is by using a CSS animation to animate the `background-position` property.

The first thing we'll do is specify the keyframes for our CSS animation. Add the following style rule just below your `#spriteContainer` style rule:

```
@keyframes sprite {
  100% {
    background-position: -7224px;
  }
}
```

Our animation keyframes are called `sprite`, and we have only one keyframe defined. This keyframe has an identifier of `100%`, which specifies what the animation's final behavior should be. That behavior is to set the `background-position` property's horizontal position to a negative value. *This value determines by how much the sprite image needs to be shifted to the left,* and it is almost always the full width of your sprite sheet. Depending on the tool used to generate your sprite sheet, you may need to do some manual adjustments. The blue circles sprite sheet is 7,500 pixels wide, but after some unused space is removed, the actual size to shift the image by is 7,224 pixels. The negative of that is what you see as the value for the `background-position` property.

The last step is to actually define the CSS animation. In your `sprite Container` style rule, add the following line:

```
#spriteContainer {
    width: 300px;
    height: 300px;
    display: block;
    background-image: url("images/sprites_final.png");
    animation: sprite .3s ease-in infinite;
}
```

We define our CSS animation using the `animation` property, specifying our `sprite` keyframes collection, a duration of `.3` seconds,
the `ease-in` easing function, and a loop value of `infinite`. This is a
formal way of saying that we want to play our `sprite` keyframes
over a period of `.3` seconds…forever! If all of this seems bizarre to
you, check out Chapter 2 for more background.

With all of this done so far, if you preview your animation now,
you'll see an animation that just slides. What we want isn't a slide.
Instead, we want *a jump* from one frame to the other, and we'll fix
that next.

The Steps Easing Function in Action

The way are going to implement the jump is pretty simple, and it
requires using an easing function that we haven't talked much about
since we first saw it in Chapter 4. That easing function is
called `steps`:

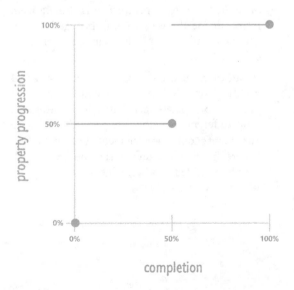

This easing function doesn't smoothly transition your properties from one value to another. Instead, it jumps between value ranges. Go ahead and use the `steps` function by modifying our animation declaration as follows:

```
#spriteContainer {
  width: 300px;
  height: 300px;
  display: block;
  background-image: url("images/sprites_final.png");
  animation: sprite .3s steps(24) infinite;
}
```

Replace the value of `ease-in` with `steps(24)`. The number 24 is important. It stands for the number of frames in our sprite sheet. For the blue circles one, if you look at it stand-alone, you'll count 24 individual instances (aka sprites). Once you've specified the number of frames as the argument to the `steps` function, test your page again. At this point, you'll see your sprites animating exactly the way you intended.

Sanity Check

If you recall, we never specified the number of pixels to slide our sprite sheet by. That is because that value is automatically calculated based on *how many pixels you are shifting left* and *how many frames your steps function is dealing with*. If you divide these two numbers together, you get the number of pixels your sprite sheet is going to be shifted by.

In our case, the division is as follows: 7,224 / 24 = 301. Our CSS animation shifts the sprite image by 301 pixels each frame. This number is a bit different than the 300-pixel size we gave our `spriteContainer` element, but that's OK. Where did this extra one pixel come from? Flash may have added it when generating the sprite. Who knows. #math

Conclusion

At this point, if you've been following my example closely, your final markup should look something like this:

```html
<!DOCTYPE html>
<html>

<head>
  <title>CSS Sprite Animation</title>
  <style>
    #spriteContainer {
      width: 300px;
      height: 300px;
      display: block;
      background-image: url("images/sprites_final.png");
      animation: sprite .3s steps(24) infinite;
    }

    @keyframes sprite {
    100% {
      background-position: -7224px;
    }
    }
  </style>
</head>

<body>
  <div id=spriteContainer></div>
</body>

</html>
```

Conceptually, animating sprites is pretty straightforward. You are basically emulating a filmstrip. Translating the concepts into something your browsers can handle is where your now ninja-like mastery of concepts like CSS animations and the steps easing function come in. Even if you never end up needing to animate sprites, you can be happy in knowing that you not only found one more practical actual use for CSS animations, but you also found a reason to use the steps easing function. How many people can lay claim to something like that? :P

CHAPTER 15

Creating a Sweet Content Slider

One of the biggest problems facing Western civilization is figuring out clever ways to display a large amount of content in a small space. One effective solution involves placing content in sequential blocks using what is known in the industry (and the 'hood) as a *content slider*. You may have never heard of it, but I'm willing to bet that you definitely have seen and used it.

To help jog your memory and to give you an idea of what you will create, navigate your browser to *http://bit.ly/content_slider*.

If you can't access a browser, here is a static example of what a content slider in its natural habitat might look like:

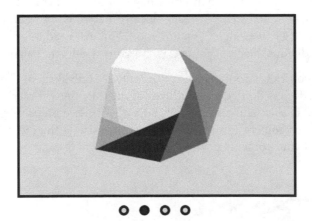

With your content slider actually loaded in your browser (or mentally with the static image), click on the circular links to see the slider in action. Depending on which link you click, the appropriate content will slide into view.

In this chapter, you will learn how to create your own sweet content slider that is very similar to this. Beyond just creating a content slider, you will learn a great deal about how the HTML, CSS, and JavaScript combine to make this example work.

Overview of How It Works

Before diving in head first and adding the HTML, CSS, and JavaScript to make it all work, let's take a step back and try to understand the big pieces that make up our content slider.

First, you have the content that you want to slide:

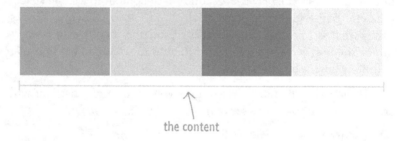

the content

Your content can be anything—images, normal HTML content, a combination, and so on. It really doesn't matter. If your content can live inside a div element, you are good. You just need to ensure that each individual block of content is the same width and height.

When you view a content slider, you only see one block of content at a time. If you don't do something about this, the entirety of your content is shamefully visible. You fix this in two steps. First, you wrap your content into a container whose size is the same as one block of your content:

the container

Once the container wraps your content, you clip the contents of everything around it to ensure only one block of your content is visible:

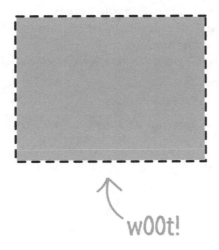

w00t!

The next step, which allows you to see the rest of your content, can be done in various ways. For this chapter, we are going to use a series of circular links that you can click:

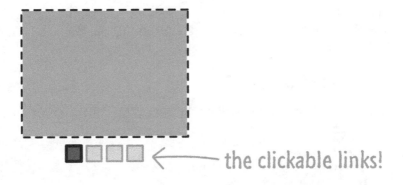

the clickable links!

The last thing is to make the actual sliding work when each link is clicked. This involves some CSS tweaks along with some JavaScript, but it is nothing too complicated. And that, my dear friends and enemies, is a high-level overview of how to make your content slider work.

In the next few sections, let's put some real HTML, CSS, and Java-Script behind this overview to bring our content slider to life.

The Content

Let's go through the steps from our overview in order…starting with the content. First, we need a starting point. Create a blank HTML document and add the following markup from the HTML5 Starting Template (*http://bit.ly/2mo2Dg2*) to it:

```
<!DOCTYPE html>
<html>

<head>
  <title>An Interesting Title Goes Here</title>

  <style>

  </style>
</head>

<body>

  <script>

  </script>
</body>

</html>
```

This markup doesn't do anything outside of just setting up our document, but it does tee us up nicely for adding our content. Let's do that next.

The Content (For Realz This Time)

Inside the body element, add the following HTML just above your script tag:

```
<div id="wrapper">
    <div id="itemOne" class="content">
```

```
    </div>
    <div id="itemTwo" class="content">

    </div>
    <div id="itemThree" class="content">

    </div>
    <div id="itemFour" class="content">

    </div>
</div>
```

Inside your `style` tags, add the following style rules to give your content some shape and color:

```
#wrapper {
  width: 2200px;
  transform: translate3d(0, 0, 0);
}
.content {
  float: left;
  width: 550px;
  height: 350px;
  white-space: normal;
  background-repeat: no-repeat;
}
#itemOne {
  background-color: #0099CC;
  background-image:
    url("https://www.kirupa.com/images/blueSquare.png");
}
#itemTwo {
  background-color: #FFCC00;
  background-image:
    url("https://www.kirupa.com/images/yellowSquare.png");
}
#itemThree {
  background-color: #FF6666;
  background-image:
    url("https://www.kirupa.com/images/pinkSquare.png");
}
#itemFour {
  background-color: #E8E8E8;
  background-image:
    url("https://www.kirupa.com/images/graySquare.png");
}
```

If you preview your page in its current state, you will see something that looks similar to the following screenshot:

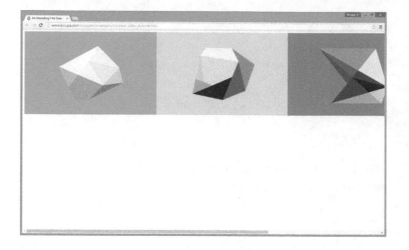

You will see four large rectangular blocks arranged neatly side by side. Depending on your screen resolution and browser size, you may need to scroll a little or a lot to see all of the squares.

At this point, take a few moments and try to understand why you see the result that you see. Take a quick look at your HTML and notice the elements that are in your document. Pay attention to the class and id values that are used, because they will correspond to the style rules you added. Speaking of which, take a look at the style rules themselves and visualize what impact they have on what is shown. Once you've done this, let's recap all of this together.

What You Just Did

In your HTML, the content that you see is made up of four div elements that all contain a class value of content. This class value maps to the .content style rule that defines the size of each of the blocks to be 550 pixels wide and 350 pixels tall:

```
.content {
  float: left;
  width: 550px;
  height: 350px;
  white-space: normal;
  background-repeat: no-repeat;
}
```

The .content style rule also specifies the float to be left. This results in your div elements lining up nicely on the same row. The last thing this style rule declares is the white-space property. This property defines how text in a paragraph will wrap. I simply provided this property as a convenience. If you decide to go beyond this chapter and add some content to each of your div items, you'll either be grateful that your text wraps appropriately or remove this property (or set it to some other value) because you don't actually want to see it.

At this point, your div element is properly sized and lined up correctly. Too bad it is completely invisible:

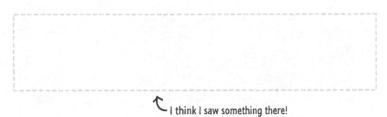

I think I saw something there!

To address this, each div is uniquely identified by an id value of itemOne, itemTwo, itemThree, and itemFour. In your style region, you have four style rules that correspond to these id values:

```
#itemOne {
  background-color: #0099CC;
  background-image:
    url("https://www.kirupa.com/images/blueSquare.png");
}

#itemTwo {
  background-color: #FFCC00;
  background-image:
    url("https://www.kirupa.com/images/yellowSquare.png");
}

#itemThree {
  background-color: #FF6666;
  background-image:
    url("https://www.kirupa.com/images/pinkSquare.png");
}

#itemFour {
  background-color: #E8E8E8;
  background-image:
    url("https://www.kirupa.com/images/graySquare.png");
}
```

As you can see, these style rules define just a background color and a background image that makes up our content. At this point, your div elements are no longer invisible. They appear as 550×350 sized rectangles with a solid color.

We are almost done here. The last thing we will look at is the mysterious div that contains an id of wrapper:

```
<div id="wrapper">
  <div id="itemOne" class="content">

  </div>
  <div id="itemTwo" class="content">

  </div>
  <div id="itemThree" class="content">

  </div>
  <div id="itemFour" class="content">

  </div>
</div>
```

This wrapper element encompasses all of our content into one single container. This isn't *the* container I was referring to in the overview that clips all of the content. That one will make its guest appearance in a little bit. No, this element's purpose is literally just to wrap the content in order to help us slide everything around.

The corresponding #wrapper style rule corroborates that story quite well:

```
#wrapper {
  width: 2200px;
  transform: translate3d(0, 0, 0);
}
```

This style rule first defines the width of the wrapper element as being 2,200 pixels. That is the total width of our content, which you get by multiplying 4 (the number of div elements) by 550 pixels. The transform property with the translate3d function set us up for being able to position this wrapper anywhere we feel like it. Because our div content blocks are children of this div, they go where the wrapper div goes. As you can imagine, this comes in quite handy in a world where things need to slide around!

Clipping the Content

In the previous section, we took care of getting our content blocks to appear. The next thing we are going to do is clip our content so that only one block of it is visible at any given time. This is where *the* container comes in. Take your HTML and wrap the entire chunk inside a div whose id is contentContainer:

```
<div id="contentContainer">
  <div id="wrapper">
    <div id="itemOne" class="content">

    </div>
    <div id="itemTwo" class="content">

    </div>
    <div id="itemThree" class="content">

    </div>
    <div id="itemFour" class="content">

    </div>
  </div>
</div>
```

Just add the two highlighted lines and, optionally, indent the lines that you just wrapped to make your HTML look properly formatted. With our content wrapped (again), you won't see anything new if you preview now. Just wrapping your elements doesn't do anything meaningful—especially not the kind of clipping-related meaning we are going for. To add that meaning, add the following #contentContainer style rule:

```
#contentContainer {
  width: 550px;
  height: 350px;
  border: 5px solid black;
  overflow: hidden;
}
```

Notice that you are sizing your contentContainer element at 550 pixels by 350 pixels. That is the exact same size as each of your content blocks. To help make the slider stand out a bit, we define a black border with a width of 5 pixels. The last thing we do, and this is the step that clips the content, is set the overflow property to hidden. This hides any content that goes outside the boundaries of the contentContainer element.

Put all of this together, and this is what you see when you preview in your browser now:

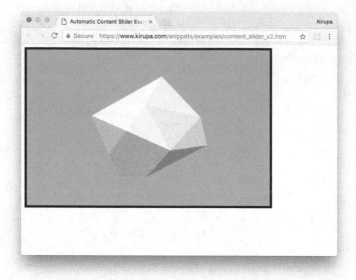

Notice that only the content from your first block is visible. The rest of your content is still there, except it is simply clipped thanks to the `overflow` property's `hidden` value. You can learn more about clipping content by looking at the Clipping Content Using CSS tutorial (*http://bit.ly/2naPUNz*) online.

The Navigation Links

We are slowly getting there! We are getting closer to having a working content slider. The next piece we are going to tackle is the navigation links—the things you click on to tell your scroller to show some different content. These links have nothing to do with your `contentContainer` or any other HTML you currently have, so go ahead and add the highlighted lines below all of the HTML you added (but above your `script` tag):

```
<div id="contentContainer">
  <div id="wrapper">
    <div id="itemOne" class="content">

    </div>
```

```
    <div id="itemTwo" class="content">

    </div>
    <div id="itemThree" class="content">

    </div>
    <div id="itemFour" class="content">

    </div>
  </div>
</div>
<div id="navLinks">
  <ul>
    <li class="itemLinks" data-pos="0px"></li>
    <li class="itemLinks" data-pos="-550px"></li>
    <li class="itemLinks" data-pos="-1100px"></li>
    <li class="itemLinks" data-pos="-1650px"></li>
  </ul>
</div>
```

Let's take a quick look at the HTML you just added. To start off, you have a div with an id of navLinks that wraps an unordered list. The links themselves are made up of list items. Each list item contains a class value of itemLinks, and each list item also contains a custom data-* attribute called data-pos. We'll revisit the data-pos attribute in a little bit.

We need to style our newly added HTML. In your style region, add the following style rules:

```
#navLinks {
  text-align: center;
  width: 550px;
}
#navLinks ul {
  margin: 0px;
  padding: 0px;
  display: inline-block;
  margin-top: 6px;
}
#navLinks ul li {
  float: left;
  text-align: center;
  margin: 10px;
  list-style: none;
  cursor: pointer;
  background-color: #CCCCCC;
  padding: 5px;
  border-radius: 50%;
  border: black 5px solid;
```

```
}
#navLinks ul li:hover {
    background-color: #FFFF00;
}
#navLinks ul li.active {
    background-color: #333333;
    color: #FFFFFF;
    outline-width: 7px;
}
#navLinks ul li.active:hover {
    background-color: #484848;
    color: #FFFFFF;
}
```

Wow, that is a lot of CSS. Despite the quantity, there isn't really anything unique or interesting going on here. Part of the CSS goes
toward making a horizontal menu with the links appearing side by
side. The rest defines the look of each link along with the corresponding hover state.

OK, there is one thing to call out. That has to do with the two style
rules that refer to an active class:

```
#navLinks ul li.active {
    background-color: #333333;
    color: #FFFFFF;
    outline-width: 7px;
}
#navLinks ul li.active:hover {
    background-color: #484848;
    color: #FFFFFF;
}
```

If you recall from your HTML, there was no element that had a
class value of active. Despite that, these style rules will eventually
get used because the active class is added to one of our links
dynamically. You'll see the madness behind this in greater detail
shortly.

At this point, your slider will look as follows:

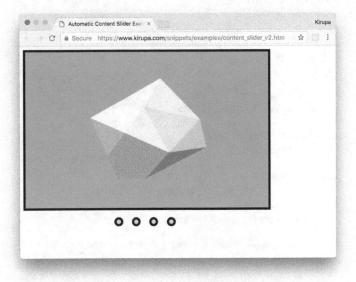

If your slider doesn't look like that, there is a very high chance that there is a typo somewhere that is causing the problems...or it could be something else. Aren't I helpful?

Making the Content Actually Slide

OK, at this point, we just have something that very convincingly looks like it should work. Clicking any of the links does absolutely nothing, though. Let's quickly get the slider into a working state by first adding our JavaScript and then adding the icing...which is a nice, frothy CSS transition.

Adding the JavaScript

Inside the `script` tag, add the following lines of JavaScript:

```
// just querying the DOM...like a boss!
var links = document.querySelectorAll(".itemLinks");
var wrapper = document.querySelector("#wrapper");

// provides a pointer to the currently displayed item
var activeLink = 0;

// set up the event listeners
for (var i = 0; i < links.length; i++) {
```

```
    var link = links[i];
    link.addEventListener("click", setClickedItem, false);

    // identify the item for the activeLink
    link.itemID = i;
}

// set first item as active
links[activeLink].classList.add("active");

function setClickedItem(e) {
  removeActiveLinks();

  var clickedLink = e.target;
  activeLink = clickedLink.itemID;

  changePosition(clickedLink);
}

function removeActiveLinks() {
  for (var i = 0; i < links.length; i++) {
    links[i].classList.remove("active");
  }
}

// Handle changing the slider position as well as ensure
// the correct link is highlighted as being active
function changePosition(link) {
  var position = link.getAttribute("data-pos");

  var translateValue = "translate3d(" + position + ", 0px, 0)";
  wrapper.style.transform = translateValue;

  link.classList.add("active");
}
```

Once you have added this, preview the page in your browser and click on any of the circular links. You will see that the slider jumps to the content corresponding to the link. Certainly, that's a whole lotta progress. All we have left is to change the sudden jump into a nice slide.

Adding the Transition

Right now, we have a content slider that doesn't actually slide to the content. It jumps to the content instead. To make our content slide, let's add a trusty transition to our slider.

Find your `#wrapper` style rule and add the following highlighted line:

```
#wrapper {
    width: 2200px;
    transform: translate3d(0, 0, 0);
    transition: transform .5s ease-in-out;
}
```

The line you added defines a transition. The properties on it specify that the transition should come to life whenever the `transform` property is modified. Your transition will run for `.5` seconds and uses an `ease-in-out` timing function to speed things up initially and slow things down toward the end.

That's all there is to animating your content slides! If you preview your document now, you should have a working content slider that slides your content when you click on any of the navigation links. This should be identical to what you saw in the example at the beginning of the chapter.

Understanding the Code (and More!)

Now that you have a content slider that works, let's try to understand how the code helps tie everything together by starting at the very beginning.

What's Really Going On

When you load your content slider, you see the first block of content displayed. The remaining content is clipped and hidden from view:

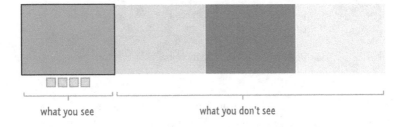

what you see   what you don't see

Clicking on each link slides your content left and right depending on which content needs to be made visible. The content slider knows which content to pull into view because of an unholy alliance forged between each navigation link and the pixel position of each block of content.

Let's try to understand this alliance. There are several things we know. We know that each of our content blocks is 550 pixels wide. We also know that our first block of content is horizontally positioned at 0 pixels. How do we know that? All of our content blocks are wrapped inside the wrapper element that snugly encloses all of our content, and the leftmost edge of the wrapper element is at 0 pixels:

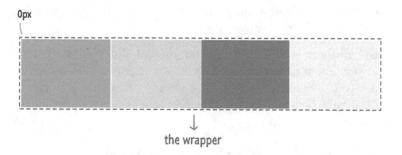

the wrapper

You can see this declared in the #wrapper style rule. We also know from that style rule that all of the content blocks float left and appear snugly in one row.

Knowing what we know, we can extrapolate the positions for all of the blocks of content as follows:

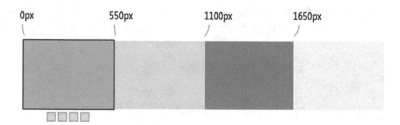

The first block is positioned at 0 pixels. One block's width away is the second block of content, at 550 pixels. Each subsequent block has a position that is 550 pixels more than the block preceding it. Because we know the exact starting pixel position for each of our content blocks, we can use that information to tell our content slider to slide the wrapper element to the right location to display the content we want.

The Role of the data-pos Attribute

At this point, you know the pixel positions of all of our content. What we still haven't discussed is *how* knowing the pixel positions of the content helps us slide the right content into view. How does clicking a link inform the content slider which content block to slide to? Simple. Each link contains the exact pixel position of the content it represents:

```
<div id="navLinks">
  <ul>
    <li class="itemLinks" data-pos="0px"></li>
    <li class="itemLinks" data-pos="-550px"></li>
    <li class="itemLinks" data-pos="-1100px"></li>
    <li class="itemLinks" data-pos="-1650px"></li>
  </ul>
</div>
```

Take a look at the `data-pos` attribute for each of the links, and notice its value. These values are the negative of the starting horizontal position of each of our content blocks. When each link is clicked, we use some JavaScript to read the `data-pos` attribute associated with the clicked link and then shift our wrapper element by the pixel value stored inside it.

For example, here is what clicking the third link looks like:

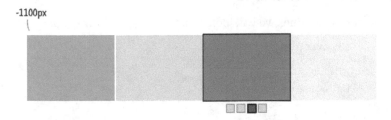

The third link specifies a `data-pos` value of –1,100 pixels. That corresponds to how many pixels we will need to shift our wrapper container to ensure the third content block appears in focus. Clicking each of the other links will set the `left` property of the wrapper element to the value stored by the clicked link's `data-pos` attribute.

OK, now you have seen the unholy alliance between the link and the position of the content I mentioned earlier. All that is left is to look at the JavaScript that converts all of the text in this section into something the browser understands.

It's All About the JavaScript

Because you have a good idea of how everything works inside our content slider, the JavaScript you are about to see should map nicely to what you know. As I try to do with many of these examples, let's go through each line of JavaScript and look at how it helps make our content slider work.

Let's start at the very top:

```
var links = document.querySelectorAll(".itemLinks");
var wrapper = document.querySelector("#wrapper");
```

The links variable gets a collection of all the elements in our document that have a class value of itemLinks. These elements are the list items that act as our navigation links. The wrapper variable is very similar. It gets a pointer to the element whose id is wrapper.

You will see both of these variables used shortly, so don't forget about them.

The next line is a bit mysterious:

```
var activeLink = 0;
```

The activeLink variable is used to store the position of the content that is currently displayed. This variable will make more sense when I describe it in action shortly.

The next set of lines we will look at is the following for loop:

```
// set up the event listeners
for (var i = 0; i < links.length; i++) {
  var link = links[i];
  link.addEventListener("click", setClickedItem, false);

  link.itemID = i
}
```

What we are doing here is going through each item in our links variable and assigning an event listener to it. This event listener will call the setClickedItem function when the click event is overheard.

The next line causes a whole host of changes:

```
// set first item as active
links[activeLink].classList.add("active");
```

We add the `active` class value to our first navigation link element by passing in the `activeLink` value to our `links` array. Because `active Link` is 0, this is essentially getting the first element and using the `classList` API to add a class value of `active`.

Once this line executes, remember the following style rules?

```
#navLinks ul li.active {
  background-color: #333333;
  color: #FFFFFF;
  outline-width: 7px;
}
#navLinks ul li.active:hover {
  background-color: #484848;
  color: #FFFFFF;
}
```

Well, these style rules now become active and help special-case your active navigation link from the other inactive links. We'll revisit these style rules again with a bit more detail.

The next thing we will look at is the `setClickedItem` event handler that gets called when you click on any of the links:

```
function setClickedItem(e) {
  removeActiveLinks();

  var clickedLink = e.target;
  activeLink = clickedLink.itemID;

  changePosition(clickedLink);
}
```

This function first resets all of your links to their inactive state by calling `removeActiveLinks`. We'll look at that function a bit later. The other important thing this function does is update the value of `activeLink` by the clicked element's `itemID` property. This ensures that `activeLink` is always pointing to a number that corresponds to what is shown.

Once it has done these two (pretty boring) things, this function passes a reference to the clicked element to the `changePosition` function, which does a couple of pretty awesome things:

```
// Handle changing the slider position as well as ensure
// the correct link is highlighted as being active
function changePosition(link) {
  var position = link.getAttribute("data-pos");
```

```
    var translateValue = "translate3d(" + position + ", 0px, 0)";
    wrapper.style[transformProperty] = translateValue;

    link.classList.add("active");
}
```

Specifically, the changePosition function:

1. Toggles the visuals of the clicked link to indicate it is currently the active one.
2. Sets the position of the wrapper element.

Let's examine these steps in greater detail.

Toggling the visuals of the clicked/active link

To expand on what I mentioned earlier, your navigation links can be in one of two states to help you figure out which content is currently active:

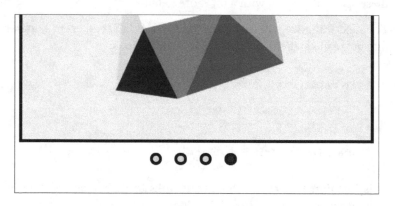

You can quickly see that the content block for the fourth link is the active one, and that the first three links are not active. We implement this change in the visuals by adding and removing CSS classes. A class called active is added to the active link. Any links that are not active do not have the active class as part of their class value. We strictly enforce that, as you will see when we look at the removeActiveLinks function.

In an earlier section, you may recall that we called out the following two style rules:

```
#navLinks ul li.active {
  background-color: #333333;
  color: #FFFFFF;
```

```
    outline-width: 7px;
}
#navLinks ul li.active:hover {
    background-color: #484848;
    color: #FFFFFF;
}
```

These style rules apply only to the link that has the active class added to it. The way this class value gets added and removed is entirely through JavaScript when a link is clicked. In our setClicke dItem function (aka the function that gets called as a result of clicking on a link), we call removeActiveLinks first:

```
function setClickedItem(e) {
    removeActiveLinks();

    var clickedLink = e.target;
    activeLink = clickedLink.itemID;

    changePosition(clickedLink);
}
```

This function is responsible for removing the active class from all of our navigation links:

```
function removeActiveLinks() {
    for (var i = 0; i < links.length; i++) {
        links[i].classList.remove("active");
    }
}
```

Think of it as a giant reset switch. It goes through each of the navigation links stored by the links variable and removes the active class value by using classList.remove(). Just know that if any of your navigation links have a class value that contains active, well... it won't have to deal with that anymore.

So, we looked at how to remove your active class from all of your links. The adding step happens very easily, as shown in the following highlighted line inside our changePosition function:

```
function changePosition(link) {
    var position = link.getAttribute("data-pos");

    var translateValue = "translate3d(" + position + ", 0px, 0)";
    wrapper.style[transformProperty] = translateValue;

    link.classList.add("active");
}
```

The `classList` that we used earlier to remove the `active` class value is the same one we use to add the `active` class value back to the clicked link. This clicked link is represented by the `link` argument that is passed in.

Setting the position of the wrapper

We are almost done! After all of this waiting and anticipation, we are finally at the part of the `changePosition` function where we actually set the position of the wrapper element to slide and display the content whose navigation link you clicked.

Let's look at the highlighted lines:

```
function changePosition(link) {
    var position = link.getAttribute("data-pos");

    var translateValue = "translate3d(" + position + ", 0px, 0)";
    wrapper.style.transform = translateValue;

    link.classList.add("active");
}
```

The `position` variable stores the value from our clicked link's `data-pos` attribute. Once we have the value of our `data-pos` attribute, we set the `transform` CSS property on the wrapper element directly to that value in the form of a `translate3d` function. These are the values that you pass in that determine how far to slide the slider.

We are almost done here. This time, I'm actually serious. We just looked at how the position is changed. How does this give you the sliding effect where the position change is animated? Do you remember what we added to the `#wrapper` style rule just a short while ago? The important line from that style rule is highlighted here:

```
#wrapper {
    width: 2200px;
    transform: translate3d(0, 0, 0);
    transition: transform .5s ease-in-out;
}
```

Notice that we have defined a transition to kick into high gear when the `transform` property is modified. Guess what our JavaScript is doing? You are setting the `transform` property! Your CSS transition detects this change and takes care of sliding your content. All you had to do was add a few lines of JavaScript (and many lines of vendor prefixing fun!) to make it all work. I don't know about you, but I think that is just amazing. This is something that you couldn't have imagined doing a few years ago without having to exert a lot of effort and write code to handle the actual sliding. This is what makes our content slider sweet.

Is All This Code Necessary?

I don't know. Does a peacock really need all its feathers?!! In all seriousness, there are ways to simplify this code quite a bit if all you care about is using the four small circles to help you to navigate through this slider. If you go further and add a timer (for a slideshow) or add back and forward arrows, you'll find that some of these helper functions and our slightly verbose way of sliding will turn out to be pretty helpful. To see for yourself, see my tutorial "Bonus: Automatic Content Slider" (*https://www.kirupa.com/html5/ creating_a_sweet_content_slider.htm#sliderStart*) to learn how to turn our slider into a slideshow!

Conclusion

So, there you have it—a look at how to create a sweet content slider using just a little bit of HTML, CSS, and JavaScript. Beyond that, you learned how to make some modifications to help the slider perform better or slide automatically. While the amount of markup and code you had to write was light, the concepts you had to know were a bit on the heavy side.

Content sliders come in many shapes and sizes and forms. Some are made up of multiple rows with the sliding happening both vertically and horizontally. Some are vertically aligned with the content in a stack. If you are adventurous and would like to use a CSS animation instead of a transition, you can do that as well with a certain amount of hacking. There is no wrong way to create a content slider. As long as your content slides, you are OK in my book!

CHAPTER 16

Conclusion

Phew! As you may have noticed, there aren't too many pages left to go. That can only mean one thing. You are reaching the end of this book. In the last many chapters we have looked at several animation-related topics together, and we've covered a lot of ground:

My goal in writing this book was to help you learn enough about web animations to be effective in bringing your UIs to life. To help you achieve that, we started with the basics of using *CSS animations*

and *CSS transitions*, and then we made things a bit more interesting by throwing some *JavaScript techniques* into the mix. Those three ingredients made up the entirety of the important concepts you learned and had to remember. Everything else we looked at just combined these three ingredients into interesting combinations. We looked at a bunch of examples, figured out exactly how they work, and then built upon our knowledge with something a little cooler and a little bit more complex in the next chapter. Hopefully those examples taught you something new and inspired you with ideas on how you can apply them for your own projects.

Until Next Time

I really *really* hope you found this book informative as well as enjoyable (aka *infoyable*). If you have any technical questions or just need to bounce some ideas off your peers, post on the forums at *http://forum.kirupa.com*. For all other types of questions or comments, feel free to contact me directly. You can tweet to *@kirupa* or send me an e-mail at *kirupa@kirupa.com*.

And with that...we'll catch up again soon!

Cheers,

Index

performance
number of elements rendered by
GPU affecting, 48
number of transition properties
affecting, 70, 80
of parallax scrolling, 151
properties negatively affecting, 47
properties positively affecting,
45-46, 50
requestAnimationFrame function
optimizing, 63-64
of scroll-activated animations,
122-124
position property, 47
properties, vii
(see also specific properties)
animation-friendly, 45-46, 50
animation-unfriendly, 47
animation-unsupported, 79
changing in CSS (keyframe) animations, 70
changing in CSS transitions, 69
changing using JavaScript, 57-60
listening for all properties
changed, 27, 28, 70, 80
names of, in JavaScript, 60

R
rendering, performing on GPU, 45,
47-51
requestAnimationFrame function,
62-64
RGBA values, 80
right property, 47
rotate function, 26, 27, 131
rotations
modifying transformation point
of, 128-131
randomizing, 132-134

S
scale function, 67-67, 88-89
scale3d function, 26, 27
scaling text, 85-91
scripted animations (see JavaScript)
scroll event, 115-116, 122
scroll-activated animations

active elements, styling, 112-114
detecting scrolling, 115-116
overview, 107-111
performance of, 122-124
visibility of elements, determining, 109-111, 116-117
scrolling with parallax effect (see parallax scrolling)
scrollX property, 147
scrollY property, 147
setInterval function, 63
setTimeOut function, 63
sliders, content (see content sliders)
sliding menus
event listeners for, 101, 103
initial page for, 97-99
menu for, hiding, 102-103
menu for, making topmost in z-
index, 105
menu for, scrolling, 103-105
menu for, showing, 99-101,
101-102
overview, 93-97
smooth animations
animation-friendly properties for,
45-46
creating, 45-51
overview, 44-45
rendering elements on GPU, 45,
47-51
responsiveness of, 44
speed of, 44
sprite sheet animations
div element for viewport, 155-156
overview, 153-155
sprite sheet, creating, 154-155
sprite sheet, setting as background
image, 156-157
sprite sheet, shifting, 157-159
sprite sheet, stepping through,
159-160
start and end states of animation, 5-6
steps function, 39-40, 159-160
stopPropagation method, 103
style object, 60
styles, vii
(see also properties)
changing using JavaScript, 57-60

About the Author

Kirupa Chinnathambi has spent most of his life trying to teach others to love web development as much as he does.

In 1999, before *blogging* was even a word, he started posting tutorials on *kirupa.com*. In the years since then, he has written hundreds of articles, written a few books (none as good as this one), recorded a bunch of videos you can find on YouTube, and currently helps make the web a better place for developers as a Program Manager at Microsoft. When he isn't writing or talking about web development, he is probably sleeping...or writing about himself in third person.

Colophon

The animal on the cover of *Creating Web Animations* is a Spix's macaw (*Cyanopsitta spixii*), named after naturalist Johann von Spix. This bird is believed to be extinct in the wild, though there was a sighting in June 2016—the first since 2000. Around 130 macaws are in captivity, and biologists hope to breed and eventually reintroduce them to their native environment. Spix's macaws used to live in dry forest habitat in Brazil, and were highly dependent on one species of tree (the silver trumpet tree) for nesting and food. This made them extremely vulnerable to habitat destruction.

These birds have blue feathers (shading from grey-blue on their head to a darker blue on their torso, wings, and tail), and grey faces. They are a medium-sized parrot at around 300 grams in weight and an average of 56 cm in length. Their diet is made up of nuts and seeds. Spix's macaws have elaborate courtship rituals that include flying together and feeding their partner.

The Spix's macaw was featured in the 2011 animated film *Rio*.

Many of the animals on O'Reilly covers are endangered; all of them are important to the world. To learn more about how you can help, go to *animals.oreilly.com*.

The cover image is an illustration by Karen Montgomery, based on an engraving from Cassell's *Natural History*. The cover fonts are URW Typewriter and Guardian Sans. The text font is Adobe Minion Pro; the heading font is Adobe Myriad Condensed; and the code font is Dalton Maag's Ubuntu Mono.

Learn from experts.
Find the answers you need.

Sign up for a **10-day free trial** to get **unlimited access** to all of the content on Safari, including Learning Paths, interactive tutorials, and curated playlists that draw from thousands of ebooks and training videos on a wide range of topics, including data, design, DevOps, management, business—and much more.

Start your free trial at:
oreilly.com/safari

(No credit card required.)

CPSIA information can be obtained
at www.ICGtesting.com
Printed in the USA
LVHW06s2050280318
571476LV00005B/49/P